Routledge Revivals

NERVES AND PERSONAL POWER

NERVES

AND

PERSONAL POWER

SOME PRINCIPLES OF PSYCHOLOGY AS APPLIED TO CONDUCT AND HEALTH

By

D. MACDOUGALL KING, M.B.

Author of "The Battle with Tuberculosis and How to Win It."

WITH INTRODUCTION BY
Rt. HON. W. L. MACKENZIE KING

Routledge
Taylor & Francis Group

First published in 1922 by Fleming H. Revell Co.

This edition first published in 2018 by Routledge
2 Park Square, Milton Park, Abingdon, Oxon, OX14 4RN
and by Routledge
711 Third Avenue, New York, NY 10017

Routledge is an imprint of the Taylor & Francis Group, an informa business

Publisher's Note
The publisher has gone to great lengths to ensure the quality of this reprint but points out that some imperfections in the original copies may be apparent.

Disclaimer
The publisher has made every effort to trace copyright holders and welcomes correspondence from those they have been unable to contact.
A Library of Congress record exists under ISBN: 23001037

ISBN 13: 978-1-138-55357-6 (hbk)
ISBN 13: 978-1-138-56738-2 (pbk)
ISBN 13: 978-0-203-70300-7 (ebk)

NERVES
AND PERSONAL POWER

NERVES
AND
PERSONAL POWER

SOME PRINCIPLES OF PSYCHOLOGY AS APPLIED TO CONDUCT AND HEALTH

By

D. MACDOUGALL KING, M. B.

Author of "The Battle with Tuberculosis and How to Win It."

WITH INTRODUCTION BY

Rt. HON. W. L. MACKENZIE KING

NEW YORK CHICAGO

Fleming H. Revell Company

LONDON AND EDINBURGH

New York: 158 Fifth Avenue
Chicago: 17 North Wabash Ave.
London: 21 Paternoster Square
Edinburgh: 75 Princes Street

Introduction

> "Who, doom'd to go in company with Pain,
>
> . . . .
>
> Turns his necessity to glorious gain;"
>
> —Wordsworth—*The Happy Warrior.*

MY brother, Dr. D. Macdougall King, was practising his profession in the city of Ottawa when, at the age of thirty-five, he was stricken suddenly with influenza complicated by double pneumonia. Tuberculosis of the acute type manifested itself after this attack. It spread rapidly to every lobe of the lungs. So virulent was the disease that its appearance seemed to make thought of recovery all but impossible.

The circumstances surrounding this illness were particularly distressing. Only a year or two before, my brother had assumed the responsibilities of a home and to these had been added, within a few months prior to his breakdown, the parentage of twin sons. Being himself a physician, he was under no delusion as to the significance of the attack. I vividly recall the alternatives as he depicted them to me in the spring of 1913. He might live until the autumn; that depended on just how virulent the disease was, and how strong his power of resistance. He might, with great care and under the most favourable conditions, survive a period of complete invalidism of from two to three years, and possibly some day resume the practice of medicine, though enfeebled for the remainder of his days. That depended on his regaining sufficient strength to permit of a journey to Colorado and his assuming permanent residence there. Was it worth while to make the attempt, and how make it with no resources at his command? One cannot fight tuberculosis on one's own. Being himself a physician he knew; and he knew all. That was the appalling feature of the situation. Except for his wife and little ones, I doubt if his brave spirit would have debated the issue; but for his wife, I doubt if it could have, for long. For her sake he determined to make the fight, and through her never-failing ministrations he was enabled to win it.

The home in Ottawa was broken up. My brother became a patient in the sanitorium at Ste. Agathe, in the Province of Quebec, and, later, in the Agnes (Phipps) Memorial Sanitorium in Denver, Colorado. For most of this period, extending considerably over a year, neither he nor his wife saw anything of their children. From the sanitorium, he was moved to a cottage in Denver, where the little family was re-united. There, through tenderest care, and after confinement to bed for yet another year, the reward of the long period of absolute rest began to make itself felt. The fight was far from over, but the disease became quiescent, and health and strength returned in imperceptible stages. During the third year, the disease had become so quiescent as to cause my brother to feel that, though unable to resume active practice, he was nevertheless justified in attempting to make a contribution to the literature of his profession which he hoped might prove of service to fellow-sufferers. With his knowledge as a physician, supplemented by the facts and observations of his own tragic experience, he commenced the writing of a book entitled *The Battle with Tuberculosis and How to Win It.**

During the South African War, my brother served with the British forces as a member of the Canadian Army Medical Corps. This experience he sought to turn to account in the treatise on tuberculosis. He believed that once a patient could be brought to see that like rewards wait upon courage and discipline, whether the battle be against a human foe, or against disease as one of the common enemies of mankind, the humblest private in the ranks of human sufferers might come to recognize himself a general commanding the forces of life in their resistance of the legions of death. Making use of the analogies which military training and tactics afford, he sought to supply the motif essential to sustained effort, and, in language every

* *The Battle with Tuberculosis and How to Win It,* (1917) J. B. Lippincott Company, Philadelphia.

layman could understand, to unfold, with scientific accuracy, the strategy of war against disease.

There was yet another purpose in this method of treatment of the subject of tuberculosis. Because of his illness, my brother had been deprived of all possibility of active service in the Great War. He knew full well what, as a consequence of war, the toll of tuberculosis was likely to be. Indeed, it was through exposure and illness in South Africa that his own physical constitution was first weakened and thereby rendered a prey to subsequent infections. His aim was to help those who, like himself, had known something of active service in the field, and who, through the vicissitudes of war, might be brought into single-handed conflict against disease. He had experienced and understood the contrast, facing death in action with a world on-looking, and facing it in a long drawn-out battle of inaction, in isolation, and with none of war's recognitions or rewards. In his high purpose he succeeded beyond expectation. He lived to receive from more than one military hospital, and from many an invalided soldier, expressions of profoundest gratitude.

The writing of the book on tuberculosis was proceeded with, necessarily, very slowly. Undue intellectual effort is just as perilous in the recovery from tuberculosis as excess of physical effort. For the greater part of a year, the most he dared venture, by way of either research or composition, was from a fraction of an hour to an hour twice a day. Part of the book was written while he was lying on his back; much of it was dictated from his bed. In this, as in all else, his wife was constantly at his side. Within two years the manuscript was finished. In its introduction, written as most introductions are, when the volume itself is otherwise complete, my brother, referring to the extent of his recovery, was able to say: "Now, just four years since the disease made its appearance, it has become so quiescent as to permit of a limited amount of work, and life would seem to hold for the writer the prospect of years of personal happiness and also of service to his fellow-sufferers."

Those were years of increasing happiness. The night of despair had gone, and the darkest clouds were rapidly disappearing. The dawn of a new day seemed at hand Fear had been overcome by faith. Well do I remember the joyous announcement which came in June, 1916, in one of my brother's letters, that on the 14th of that month he had received five dollars in payment of professional services. This was the first money he had been able to earn since the early spring of 1913. In the month of December, 1917, his book made its appearance in print. He continued steadily to regain some measure of health and strength. Even before the publication of the book, he was able, once more, formally to announce himself as a consulting physician, and, upon occasions, to visit patients in their homes.

For a time it looked as if the service, for the opportunity for which he had fought so bravely, was to be of some duration. He had been spared to see his little lads enter upon their schooling, and, as occasion afforded, to interest himself in their early training and behaviour. With the larger freedom which his restored health permitted, the circle of his friends and interests widened. He became again the citizen, as well as the head of the household and the physician. It is not to be supposed that these days were without their uncertainties. Though the skies were no longer over-cast, they were never wholly free from some fleeting cloud. Not an hour passed which did not have its rigidly imposed restraints. Sacrifices and denials, however, were not viewed as fetters; they were looked upon, rather, as the safeguards of a new-born freedom.

When I visited my brother in the autumn of 1917, he had so far regained his health as to be able to drive a motor-car through the streets of Denver. His practice had been resumed, and he was full of hope, quiet confidence, and cheer. The two years immediately succeeding passed without much occasion for concern. Suddenly, in the midsummer of 1919, without warning or apparent cause, he experienced a physical weakness which was accompanied by a contraction of the muscles of his right hand. The symptoms were clear and unmistakable. He diagnosed the trouble as progressive muscular atrophy, owing its origin to some organic nerve degeneration. This diagnosis was subsequently confirmed by fellow physicians.

Here was a battle of another order. Tuberculosis could be successfully fought, but not progressive muscular atrophy. It left no margin for hope; it presaged the slow approach of death. Once more, being a physician, he knew; and he knew all. Again there were alternatives in the prospect that presented itself, the acceptance or rejection of either of which lay largely with himself. He could cease work altogether, intellectual as well as physical effort, and so arrest the disease and hope to live on, possibly for years; or, while compelled to abandon the practice of his profession, he could persist in intellectual work with the certainty, however, that every hour's effort would hasten the progress of the disease. He might well have faltered at such a choice. He never wavered, but, what was more, he never murmured. Prolonged idleness was to him unthinkable, unless as a part of a fight with some promise of victory at the close. Such was the case in the battle with tuberculosis. He knew that with muscular atrophy, it could not be the same. One form of victory alone was possible, and that the triumph of spirit over unconquerable odds. Again to pass on to fellow-sufferers and his profession some benefit from his own tragic experience, he determined upon the writing of another book which, by actual calculation of months, he believed he could complete before the end came. Out of this brave resolve was born the present treatise on " Nerves and Personal Power."

My brother entered upon the writing of this book with a full knowledge of all that the task implied. In one respect, the process was just the reverse of what it had been in the writing of the other book. There he began with fractions of hours, and worked up to portions of days of sustained effort. There he was experiencing, from month to month, the exhilaration of returning strength, and the promise of renewed activity. Here he began in such fullness of strength as he had regained: to work, first, with comparative freedom of movement; then, crippled and bed-ridden; finally, with complete paralysis of the greater part of his entire body. All the while he faced, knowingly, not the possibility of restored life, but the certainty of rapidly approaching death. Before the end came, in the spring of 1922, he was unable to hold a pen or to dictate a paragraph; but he had completed his self-imposed task. His last days, ever with the assistance and constant ministrations of his wife, were given over to attempts at revision of the manuscript and to correspondence concerning its publication.

It has been truly said that it takes most courage to fight a losing fight. But it takes something more than courage to continue to smile at death when it thwarts and shackles at every step of its approach. When I saw my brother in September of 1920, he was well under way with the writing of his second book. He was then slightly paralyzed and confined to his bed. Anything more wonderful or beautiful than the radiance of his spirit, I have never known. Two months later, I retraced my steps to pay him a second visit, perchance that I might learn something more of the secret of his serenity. He spoke in the most direct manner of his new affliction, and in no uncertain terms of its probable course and duration. But there was neither bitterness nor complaint in his utterance. His spirit seemed to have surmounted all there was of infirmity in his physical condition. I understand now what is meant when we are told that "patient endurance is God-like," and I think I have learned something of the love that is stronger than death.

In the preface to *The Battle with Tuberculosis,* seeking to relate his own personal experience to the craving for understanding on the part of others likewise afflicted, my brother wrote, as already quoted: "Life would seem to hold for the writer the prospect of years of personal happiness and also of service to his fellow-sufferers." In the preface to the present volume, from like motive, after referring to the bedridden and crippled condition which progressive muscular atrophy had brought about, he says, concerning himself: "Although he has been thus deprived of many of the pleasures of life, happiness has seemed to him with each passing year a greater reality. The secret of happiness, as the author conceives it, is set forth in the pages which follow."

It is the Happy Warrior who speaks in each instance: the one, a winning, the other, a losing fight. Happiness lies at the heart of both utterances. True, in the one, it is a happiness looking out upon the future, while, in the other, it is a happiness looking back upon the past. Nevertheless, in both it is a present and an abiding happiness.

I have made mention of the circumstances under which this book was written in order that its pages may not lack the authority they are entitled to possess. It contains no idle words. Every thought it expresses has had its worth tested in the fiery furnace of affliction. Its tone, nevertheless, is not austere; it is persuasive and kindly throughout. It brings the physician's touch of hope and healing to those who out of their weakness would be made strong. Apart altogether from the scientific value of the treatise, to know of the suffering which inspired its conception and the fortitude which made possible its publication, is to glimpse something of those higher levels of human greatness to which men and women are capable of rising in adversity, and which uplift all who pause to dwell upon the secret of spiritual attainment in human lives.

W. L. MACKENZIE KING.

Ottawa.
July 28, 1922.

Preface

THE aim of this treatise is to give to the public a much needed understanding of those factors in every day living which on the one hand tend toward nervous weakness, and on the other make for personal power.

From the author's viewpoint, everybody at times suffers from symptoms which are popularly termed "nervous," for nervousness is a matter of degree rather than of kind. Whether "nerves" take the form of unreasonable impulsiveness or of serious obsessions occasioning body pain, the fundamental cause and radical cure of both are essentially the same.

It is realized that nervous invalids who most urgently require the teachings of this book, unfortunately will be those least likely to derive *direct* benefit from it. In the treatment of even the most serious functional neuroses, however, there comes a time when the patient is ready for a closer knowledge than the physician has time to convey, of the reasons underlying nervous disability, and of the course to be followed to prevent a relapse. To all such sufferers, as well as to those entrusted with the care of nervous invalids, it is hoped the book will make a special appeal.

A scientific consideration of the cause and prevention of mental suffering should form a *sinè qua non* of social service and religious guidance. The author hopes that the material here assembled from philosophy, psychology, psychiatry, and other sources having a direct bearing on this border line subject, may not only give to social workers and religious teachers a similar point of view, but may also be an incentive to deeper and more serviceable reading. It may be also that because of its importance in medico-legal controversies, the non-technical explanation of the functional nervous diseases will prove helpful to members of the legal profession.

In any discussion, however limited, of the great mysteries of the mind, it is, at this early period in the development of psychology, inevitable that the theories advanced should be critically viewed by those whose study, or lack of study, may have led them to other conclusions. The author has sought to be as little disturbing as possible to those who have a working philosophy of life. To any who are yet unsatisfied, the theories of mind advanced by William James and William McDougall, and briefly touched upon and applied in this book, seem to afford a basis of reality at once tangible, rational, and integrating.

It may be helpful to the reader who craves understanding in his disability, to know that the author, through personal experience, realizes something of the point of view of a sufferer. After successfully waging a battle with tuberculosis for over five years, he has become crippled and bedridden as the result of an organic nerve degeneration causing progressive muscular atrophy. Although he has been thus deprived of many of the pleasures of life, happiness has seemed to him with each passing year a greater reality. The secret of happiness as the author conceives it, is set forth in the pages which follow.

D. M. K.

Denver, Colo.

Contents

PART I—FACTS

PART II—FACTS IGNORED

CONTENTS

PART III—FACTS APPLIED

PART I

FACTS

I

"NERVES" AND THE PREMISES

THERE is no denying that the last doctor consulted made a thorough examination, and, like the others, he has said: "There is nothing organically wrong; it is only 'nerves.'" Somehow the thought always seems to be implied that there is *nothing* really wrong, that it is all imagination, and to say the least, this is disheartening, because you and I *know* there is something very much wrong, and we realize that unless we discover what that something is, and take definite steps to correct it, we must continue the increasingly unhappy existence which has become daily bondage.

First of all, let us carefully examine the doctor's statement. He has said, "Nothing *organically* wrong." Just what does this mean? Let us suppose, as an illustration, that you frequently have trouble with your telephone. It buzzes and crackles, sometimes the conversation is cut off, frequently you are given the wrong number, or you find there are several parties trying to get a hearing at the same time. After repeated complaints, the trouble department comes to the conclusion that there may be something radically wrong, and it sends out a lineman to examine systematically the telephone, the batteries, the wires, the big cables, the switchboard, in short, every part of the mechanism. You know for a fact that the lineman is an expert at his work, and that he will recognize trouble the moment he sees it. His report is, however, that everything is in perfect order; no broken wires, no twists in the cable, the solution in the battery quite up to normal, and each part of the works just as perfect as the day it was installed. His verdict would be, "*Nothing organically wrong.*"

Does this mean there is *nothing* wrong, that all the trouble you experience on the telephone is only imagination? Hardly. No one can deny that the confusion is marked, and the conversations are often muddled, and in spite of what anybody may say, you realize that you are not getting out of the telephone the satisfaction to which you are entitled.

Under the circumstances, being convinced that in the mechanism there is no trouble, no *organic* trouble, you are compelled to believe that the fault must lie with the personal factor of the telephone system, the central operator. We can imagine a great variety of things which might be wrong with "Central." She might not know her business!

She might be listening continually to other people's advice as to how to operate the board instead of using her own common sense. Possibly, she day dreams, or may be she simply does not wish to take the trouble! We could go on and fill pages with speculations as to what the trouble with central might be; it is enough, however, that we should realize that if the discomfort we experience with the telephone is not in the works, is not organic, it must be due to faulty methods employed by the central operator.

You have recognized, of course, the analogy between the telephone system and the nervous system. In the nervous system, the senses such as the organs of sight, hearing, smell, taste, and touch, all are telephones through which messages are sent to headquarters. The eye and ear are like telephones in very busy stations where thousands of messages are sent daily. The nerves correspond to the wires which go from each telephone, and for the greater part converge at the great cable or spinal cord which enters the brain. The brain is analogous to the main office where the central operator, who is recognizable in the moral self, carries out its function.

It is not our purpose to try to determine just how much a thing apart from the body the moral self is, but it is important that we should realize that our body mechanism can be disturbed from the way it is run, as well as from a breakdown in the works.

Illness of any kind means that the body machine, or some part of it, has ceased to carry out its work or function in the normal healthy manner that is to its best interests. The function of any part of the body is the purpose of that part; for example, the purpose or function of the muscles is movement; the function of the heart is to pump blood to every part of the body, and so on. The function of any part of the body may be interfered with by two classes of conditions; first, mismanagement, and second, injury. The disturbance caused by doing things which are unwise, or by neglecting other things to which attention should be given, is called functional; the disturbance caused by actual injury, is organic.

It is evident that wrong methods in connection with the management of the body, if kept up long enough, will eventually cause actual injury with change in body tissues. By means of a careful examination of the body, doctors can tell to a practical certainty whether or not there is organic injury. If there be no organic injury, the illness is functional, that is to say, there is an interference with the normal working of the body machine caused by wrong living. The human body is managed by the instincts, the intellect, and the moral self. Were the intellect well informed in everything pertaining to the body's needs and the moral self quite strong in its support of the intellect, there could be no *functional* illness of any kind.

Consider this example of a functional disability. Tommy has discovered a pound box of chocolates, and proceeds to demolish the contents without consideration of any such wizened up thing as self-control. Result: Tommy goes to bed, and the doctor who treats the nausea, etc., says, "Indigestion, caused by too many chocolates." That undoubtedly is the case, but the fact of the matter is that Tommy's stomach organically is as healthy and strong as that of an ostrich, and that part of him wherein the primary trouble lies, is not his body but his foolish self, which allowed his body to do a thing that would have put a strong man on his back. If experience, or some kind friend, does not *educate* Tommy's ego to control his appetite for chocolates, the indigestion will become just as persistent, just as chronic, as the opportunity to over-indulge. It will be a long, long time, however, before Tommy's stomach becomes diseased, that is, develops anything organically wrong.

This is all very simple, and day by day in the majority of ailments a doctor is called upon to treat, he is but adjusting the patient's central operator with a little education and persuasion, which is much more precious than pills and plasters. Strange though, is it not, how peeved the patient is, if the drugs are omitted!

It is a matter of interesting speculation as to just how much organic disease finds its origin in unintentional mismanagement, or neglect of the body. If we all were to live as we should, there perhaps would be no disease. Whether or not it be due to ourselves, our neighbors, or our ancestors, the fact is, however, that germs, malignant growths, continuous poisoning, and other things quite beyond our limited personal control, do attack the body machine and injure it—cause organic change in it.

After the damage is done, it is doubtful whether education can be of much avail in affecting diseased body tissues; the power of thought, however, is so remarkable in some of its manifestations that scientists are becoming less dogmatic in negative statements concerning it. We are at any rate on safe ground in asserting that, even in chronic *organic* disease, especially if there be nervous symptoms, and there nearly always are, a realization of the truth with regard to "nerves" may prove a wonderful help in effecting a cure, and in making life more worth living.

The doctor's statement, "nothing organically wrong," means that whatever discomfort you experience in your body or mind is not occasioned by any breakdown in the body's mechanism. There is no disease in the back, in the brain, heart, liver, stomach or in the body as a whole. All your tiredness, pains and depressing thoughts are due to imperfect functioning on the part of the body's organs. The imperfect functioning is accounted for by the way your self runs the body machine.

In other words, in your habits of living lies the *fundamental cause* of all your troubles.

One of the most important laws of medical science is that the cause, that is to say the fundamental mental cause of any disability, is the thing which, above all else, should be treated. Obviously if the cause can be removed, the symptoms will vanish. To treat pains and depression and tiredness without concerning oneself with the fundamental cause, is like smothering smoke in an effort to put out fire.

From these facts it is apparent that while medicines may temporarily alleviate the discomfort caused by a wrong way of living, a permanent cure is to be found, first, by weeding out misconceptions and replacing them with true information; and second, which is more difficult, by putting the truth into daily practice. Know also, for a fact, that every functional disability, that is, every illness where there is nothing organically wrong, *can* be cured, and *will* be cured, just as soon as the intellect understands and the moral self makes the body conform to right living principles.

The second part of the doctor's statement to the effect that it is "only nerves" which are responsible for your troubles, seems in some ways to be a contradiction to the fact that there is nothing organically wrong. It is as though the lineman in the telephone service had said, "There is nothing broken in the mechanism, it is only *wires*." Obviously, this is ridiculous, and the only excuse for the use of the term " nerves " is that the directing mind element or self belongs to the nervous system in the same way as the central operator is a part of the telephone system.

Your nerves are just as strong and perfect in every way as are the wires of the telephone system. They carry messages quite as accurately, and their function or purpose is really less easily affected than the function of other organs.

Fortunately, the diagnosis, "nerves," even if it be a misnomer, limits the great range of possible causes to something you can realize, something you can combat, something you can cure.

The life of the human body is supported and carried on by a number of clearly defined systems which work for the well-being of the individual. For example, there is the muscular system, the digestive system, the respiratory system, and so on. When illness overtakes the body, the point of attack is not the body as a whole, as many suppose, but usually just one definite system. On the other hand, it is quite exceptional for one system to be the point of attack without, sooner or later, one or more of the other systems suffering from the derangement in the first. For example, when Tommy demolished the pound of chocolates, the point of attack was the digestive system, but it was not long before the disturbed digestive system affected the muscular system and Tommy felt weak, the circulatory system and Tommy became pale, the nervous system and a rise in temperature took place.

If trouble with the digestive system causes disturbance in other systems, even more so does an untrue or distorted habit of thought and conduct affect different parts of the body. One has but to recall the analogy of the telephone system to realize how every cubic inch of the body is in intimate association with the mind through the nervous system—is literally attached to the brain with nerve threads, just as each telephone is attached to headquarters with a wire. When, therefore, the seat of trouble is in central headquarters, it is not surprising that the effects should manifest themselves in any and every part of the body to which a nerve travels.

If unhealthy mental conditions cause an upset in systems other than the nervous, of course, in its turn, that upset is capable of coming back at the nervous system and causing still more mental distress. Thus in the body there becomes established a "vicious circle"—a society for the mutual adversity of associated systems!

Such a condition sooner or later becomes intolerable, and there arises a determination to cease cavilling about persistent thoughts, tiredness, irritability, and depression, which after all, are only effects, and to grapple with the primary cause—to break in on the vicious circle at the place where it has its origin.

Anybody who tries to persuade you that the symptoms of which you complain are not real does not understand the situation. When you suffer, there is no denying that the suffering is bona fide. This, however, is not the point, and your suffering will continue just as long as you make it the chief consideration. If you are to get well, you must realize that your whole consideration must be given to the *cause* of your troubles, and that your symptoms, whatever or wherever they may be, are of so little importance in comparison with the cause, that they can be quite ignored. Doubtless from time to time the symptoms will force themselves upon your attention, but know, as surely as you are reading this book, that if you will grapple as you should with the cause, the symptoms

> "Shall fold their tents like the Arabs,
> And as silently steal away."

We start from the premises that you have had a careful examination by the doctor; that he has said that you have nothing organically wrong, or if you have organic trouble, he is treating it. He will make clear to you which symptoms are accounted for by organic body changes. All other symptoms are functional, and will, you may rest assured, disappear one by one as you comprehend and *put into practice* the principles set forth in the following pages.

II

THE NERVOUS MACHINE

WE have traced the general cause of nervousness to the place where it has its origin. We find that the trouble centres about the manner in which the moral self carries out its function or purpose. Because the moral self does not make the body carry out its work in keeping with wise principles, the body and mind are made to suffer. What, then, is the function of the moral self, and how and where is it failing to achieve what the body as a whole looks to it to do? To give a clear conception of this, it is necessary first that we should understand something of the mechanism the moral self is called upon to control.

Long, long ago, at the time which, in Genesis, is described as the fourth and fifth day or period, when living things first existed on this world, life was so comparatively simple that one can readily grasp something of the workings of the elemental nerve processes which, millions of years later, evolved into the mechanism underlying that elusive complexity we call the personality.

To-day, even as in the long ago, the most primitive living thing consists of but a single cell. While quite incapable of doing anything on its own account, the cell possesses within itself the power of repeatedly showing response to one or more of the great forces of nature which stimulate it. It is endowed with a wonderful form of energy—the energy of life.

With every response to an outside stimulus, some of the living substance of the cell is consumed. The living substance is replenished by food materials which the cell absorbs. So it is that in this microscopic unit of life may be found the same principle of income and expenditure of living energy that governs every one of the billions of living cells which make up the human body.

In the beginning, when life first materialized itself in matter, it would have been difficult to distinguish one living cell from another. As time went on, the energy of life, growing ever larger and fuller, reached out in many directions, generally with success, but sometimes with failure. Always there was division of cells, with each part retaining something of the original, but losing in one direction while gaining in another. In this way there came about a division into the vegetable and animal kingdoms, each retaining much in common but differing in tendency, the vegetable drifting toward stability, the animal toward conscious mobility.

Each body of living cells is virtually a community of co-operating units, and it is the tendency of certain groups of cells in each body more and more to become specialists in some line of work, that is, to develop a special function which will be helpful to every other group in the community. Of cells which comprise animal life, one group which lies on the outside of the body becomes somewhat hardened, and forms a protective covering which we recognize as the skin. Another group become especially concerned in the matter of movement; the cells of this group constitute muscle fibres. A third group, called nerve cells, is engaged in catching up stimuli from without, and conveying such stimuli to the muscles.

In conformity with the requirements of the special work which cells are called upon to perform, the shape, colour, and general appearance of each group, are altered and become characteristic. Under the microscope, the cells which comprise the skin call to mind the various bricks, blocks, and flag stones used in pavements. The muscle cells resemble striped elastic bands, and a nerve cell may be likened to a tree with a very long trunk or to a diminutive devil-fish which has one very long tentacle or *axon,* and a number of short tentacles called *dendrons.*

The work of the body of a nerve cell seems to be simply to keep its axons and dendrons supplied with nourishment, while the axon and dendrons afford an excellent conducting medium along which impulses travel. So long is the axon that in some cases, as in a tall man, it may extend several feet.

It is finer than the finest filament of silk, and sometimes has a few branches. When bound together in great numbers, the axons of nerve cells form a glossy white strand which is recognized by the naked eye as a nerve. A nerve has little more function than a telephone wire. Simply it is a conductor of stimuli. An electric current applied to it anywhere in its course, will give rise to an impulse which will travel along the nerve at the rate of several yards a second.

The functioning or working portion of nerve elements seems to be located at the spot where the dendrons of one nerve cell form a junction with the dendrons of another. The junction is called a *synapse.* The dendrons of two nerve cells form a synapse just as the tops of two trees might cross or intertwine their branches; or, to hold to the analogy of the devil-fish, just as two such creatures might interlace their tentacles. When an impulse of sufficient strength reaches a synapse, it touches off, as it were, another impulse or series of them.

At the point where an axon, that is, a long tentacle of the nerve cell, reaches the surface of the body, there is attached to its end a microscopic receiver for stimuli from outside the body. The receiver is called a *sense organ.* When some form of energy, as for example a touch, comes in contact with the skin, the receiver or sense organ receives the stimulus, and through a minute explosion, that is through chemical changes within itself, sends an impulse along the axon and stimulates the synapse or nerve centre to functionate.

When a nerve which enters a muscle is stimulated with an electric current or by other means, an impulse travels along the nerve into the muscle, and some of the combustible material in the muscle is touched off by the impulse; as a result the muscle contracts. It is an interesting fact that when freshly prepared frogs' legs are being cooked, it is necessary to cover the frying pan or quite possibly the legs will jump out. This is because the heat of the pan, touching the end of a nerve filament, sends a strong impulse into the leg muscles, which contract violently as a result.

In a living body an impulse starting at a sense organ always has to pass through a synapse or junction of nerve cells in its course from sense organ to muscle. It is at the junction of the nerve cells that the impulse *from* a sense organ initiates an impulse *to* a muscle. So it is that such a junction of nerve cells is called a *nerve centre.* The cell with its axon and dendrons or filaments on one side of the centre comprises the *afferent* or *sensory* path along which travels the impulse from the sense organ; the cell on the other side comprises the *efferent* or *motor* path along which travels the impulse from the nerve centre that will cause muscular contraction and movement. Such a combination of nerve cells is a working unit, and is called a *sensori-*

motor nervous arc. The special work of the sensori motor arc is to cause the muscles to react when the sense organ is stimulated.

In a large sense, the behaviour of any living creature is nothing more or less than the muscular movements of that creature. The conduct of man is made up of locomotion, speech (which also is muscular action), movements of the hands and arms, and so on. To be sure, these movements, like the letters of the alphabet, have become joined together in many forms and fashions, but just as a thesis or a beautiful poem depends on the letters of the alphabet for its expression, so the most highly complex conduct is but an integration of reflex action.

In the sensori-motor arc, the point of greatest importance for our understanding of the mind in later evolution, is what has been termed the nerve centre, or junction of the sensory and motor nerve cells. Whether or not, like a devil-fish, the nerve cell is able to draw in its short tentacles or dendrons, has not been proved, but it seems there is very often a slight break in continuity at the place where the dendrons of one cell join those of another, and that the connection varies in intimacy from time to time. It is possible that some highly specialized material lies between the approximating dendrons, and influences the facility with which impulses pass the synapses or nerve centres. In any event, the synapse always is somewhat resistant to the passage of impulses, and is sometimes particularly so.

The resistance of the synapse to the passage of impulses, is affected permanently by some influences, and temporarily by others. Every time an impulse goes through the synapse, a molecular change takes place in it so that there is a permanent lowering of resistance to the passage of subsequent impulses. Impulses often repeated would seem in this way to create an energy path so that an impulse which was so small that originally it would have been blocked, gets through quite easily. Herein lies the explanation of habit, and how gradually with repetition of any kind of conduct, it becomes easier and easier for the impulses which bring about the action to find a passage.

If one impulse is not successful in passing a synapse, quite possibly another impulse of just the same strength will afford to the first the boost necessary to put it across. So it is that an unsuccessful impulse, if quickly repeated, is not lost; it waits for another stimulus, and adds itself to it. Of course the stronger the stimulus the more surely it goes through the synapse, and causes a more marked effect on the muscle. Should the impulse try to go in the backward direction, it is blocked at the synapse which thus acts as a valve allowing the current to pass only in the forward direction.

Of the temporary influences, fatigue makes the synapse more resistant to the passage of impulses, but with rest, the synapse quickly recovers. When there is a state of general excitement in the nervous elements, impulses pass more readily, and when the nerve arc has not conveyed impulses for some time, the resistance is greater. The blood supplies the nerve cells with nourishment, and if the blood contains toxins or hypnotic drugs, very naturally the synapses are affected so that they become more resistant to the passage of impulses.

In the scale of evolution, creatures of the nature of a fish worm are of higher development than the jelly-fish. The fish worm is made up of a series of segments the cells of which have assumed more highly specialized functions, and serve the community of segments as a whole. One group of cells comprises an alimentary tract, and looks after the digestion of food; another group forms a kidney, and assists in general elimination of the waste products; and a third group of cells, constituting the blood, travels to each segment or member of the community, providing it with supplies, and carrying away the by-products of combustion.

Through the connection established by means of the central cord of nerve cells, communication is established between all the sensori-motor arcs of the worm's body. It is now possible for a stimulus applied to the sense organs of any part of the body, to send impulses which will bring the muscles of any or all the segments into play. An important distinction between the action of the nerve centres and that of a loaded gun lies in the fact that whereas the gun completely discharges its energy with a single pulling of the trigger, the nerve centre is a repeater which, with one stimulus, continues to discharge impulses into the muscles so as to keep up movement until the excitement passes.

Impulses follow the energy paths of lowest resistance. The synapses which through time have been traversed the most frequently, that is, those which have the habit of conducting impulses, will allow the more feeble impulses to pass. The synapses of later origin will be resistant to all but the stronger impulses. Through frequent stimulation in unison, certain groups of sensori-motor arcs come to have synapses of mutually low resistance, and thus form themselves into a system. A characteristic of such a system of nervous energy paths is that when an impulse reaches it through any of its parts, all of the sensori-motor arcs included in the system are at once activated. This means that all of the muscles receiving impulses from the system are activated in unison and consequently made to co-operate.

There is always an undercurrent of energy flowing through nerves. It is generated in the sense organ by stimuli not strong enough to cause definite impulses and by natural changes in the nerve elements themselves. This undercurrent produces a tonic state, or condition of alertness, so that when the nerve centre receives a stimulus from one or more sense organs, the undercurrent is drained from other parts, combines with the impulse, and goes forward to the group of muscles connected with the nerve system stimulated. In this way there is secured co-ordination or orderliness of movement. We shall see later how this same principle of drainage of nervous energy renders it impossible for us to perceive two things at one time.

The behaviour of the fish worm is purely the result of the character of the stimuli which play on its sense organs. The more intensely the nerve centres are excited through the sense organs the more vigorous is the muscular reaction. The muscular action, moreover, varies in character according to the particular group of sense organs stimulated.

From the primitive type of nervous system such as that of the fish worm there evolved the more complex system of the higher animal. Through all its complexity, however, may be recognized the same functional unit—the sensori-motor arc—which receives stimuli from without, and directs impulses so that the muscular action which follows will tend to preserve the creature and adapt it to its environment. As time goes on, there is a great increase in the number and variety of sense organs, a corresponding increase in the number of muscle fibres, and more than a corresponding increase in the number of nerve paths between the two. Instead of just two nerve cells comprising a sensori-motor arc, there are relays on each side, so that an indefinite number of cells enter into both sensory and motor paths.

Conforming to the tendency on the part of body cells to specialize, in one group of cells, there ensues a deposit of lime salts, with the formation of bone tissue. The nerve centres in the cord become incased with bony rings called *vertebrae,* and in the leading segments which form the head, as the special sense organs of taste, smell, sight, and hearing, are evolved, they in turn find support and protection from bone formations. Not only do cells become specialized to carry out some function helpful to the community of cells as a whole, but in each department of service there develops still more highly specialized groups which are functioning units within a function.

So with the course of ages, the worm became a fish, and the fish evolved arms and legs, and developed into something of the nature of a frog. The amphibian frog was followed by the mammalia, of which the rabbit is an early representative. Successively something akin to a dog, and then an ape, preceded life's highest development, man.

It will be realized that, at its origin, the nervous mechanism is simply a device through which the great forces of the universe are brought to play upon the muscles of a living body, and cause the body to live and move. That the movements thus dictated to an otherwise inert mass, are such as to bring about steady development, and evolution to something finer and higher, bespeaks with an authority of fact a guiding force or a master hand that should prove a valuable supplement to faith.

In higher animals and in man, two great groups of muscles may be recognized. For the greater part, the one group is attached to the bones or skeleton and, in man, can be contracted at will. Hence this group is known as the *skeletal* or *voluntary* muscles. The second group activates the body's glands and forms part of the viscera or internal organs, like the heart, stomach, intestines, organs of reproduction and so on. They are called the *muscles of the visceral system,* or, because they can be controlled but little by the will, the *involuntary muscles.*

Likewise there may be recognized two great groups of sense organs—external and internal. There are millions of each. The sense organs on the body's surface contribute to the senses of touch, taste, smell, sight, and hearing. The internal sense organs are imbedded in the sheaths of the muscles, in the joints, and in the walls of the internal organs. So it is that these sense organs are stimulated by muscular movements and pressures, and by chemical changes within the viscera or internal organs. The sensations they produce vary in character, and some have a direct relationship to the emotions.

It is well that our attention should not be focused

too frequently on our body feelings, on those feelings arising from stimulation especially of the lower sense organs connected with the viscera, because with too much attention the sensations are liable to assume a vividness quite beyond our best interests. On the other hand, the useful development of our higher senses enables us to discriminate sensuous harmony from discord.

Every waking moment, thousands of sense organs are being stimulated. As you read, the paper and print give you sensations which you have learned to interpret as words. The noises of the life about you play upon your hearing senses. The pressure of your body on the chair which supports you, gives you a sense of security, provided the sense organs perceive that the chair is solid. The sense organs in the muscles also permit you to realize in what position your arms and legs are placed. The sense organs in the viscera are continually being stimulated. Most of the impulses generated in this way cause muscular action. Some impulses, for example those from the sense organs in the stomach, produce muscular action without sensation; others, like light, cause sensation reflexes so that the eyes blink. You are aware, however, only of those sensations upon which your attention is focused.

It is somewhat difficult to realize that sensation as we experience it, as for example in taste, or sound, or sight, is made up of several elemental sensations fused together, but there are many facts which go to support this theory. Furthermore, that on stimulation each sense organ can produce but one elemental sensation, is a fact which you can demonstrate for yourself by touching the back of your hand with the head of a pin. In one place it will feel cold, in another hot, according to the type of sense organ the pin stimulates. Again, in administering a hypodermic, in one spot the needle may go through the skin quite painlessly, while in another, if it happens to strike a sense organ for pain, it occasions considerable discomfort.

Each sense organ stands at the entrance to a sensory nerve path in which lies one special *psycho-physical* process. So it is that, although surrounded by several other kinds, each sense organ is a specialist in just one variety of elementary sensation. You can no more feel warmth through a sense organ for cold than you can hear with your nose. No matter what form the energy stimulating any one sense organ takes, the kind of sensation resulting is always the same. For example, cutting of the optic nerve produces flashes of light and not pain, or stimulation of the tongue with an electric current produces taste, and the taste varies according to the part of the tongue stimulated.

People generally suppose that sensation takes place where the stimulus starts on its course to the brain, that is, at the sense organ. Strange as it may seem, we really feel, taste, see, and hear, in our brain, and not in our fingers, tongue, eye, and ear. Furthermore, all sensations which have to do with any one sense, receive their origin in localized areas in the brain—areas which are well-defined and separated from each other. So it is we have the visual or sight area at the posterior of the brain, the auditory or hearing area in the temporal lobe just above the ear, and so on.

That sensation occurs in the brain, and not where it is felt, is proved by the fact that removal of a piece of the brain deprives one of all sensation corresponding to the brain area removed. For example, if the area of brain cortex corresponding to sight were cut out of the brain, blindness would result, notwithstanding that the eyes were in perfect condition. Again, by stimulating sensory nerves in the stump of an arm or leg, from which the foot or hand has been amputated, one will experience sensations which appear to be in the absent foot or hand that long since has been buried!

There is good reason to suppose that many parts of the body are supplied with sense organs the stimulation of which gives rise to general feelings of well-being or discomfort. Closely related to such feelings are *organic sensations* brought about by impulses from the sense organs embedded in the internal organs. They give rise to feelings of appetite and satiation, and disturbances like colic, palpitation, faintness and so on. When subjected to frequent attention through body introspection, some of these sensations from the internal organs come to play altogether too important a rôle in some individuals.

Closely related to organic sensation is *emotion.* To understand the mechanism of emotion, we must realize that its purpose is to assist in adapting living creatures to their environment, and that it has fulfilled this purpose throughout the ages of evolution. Take, for example, the emotion of fear. It is essentially a feeling or desire favourable to flight and its purpose, especially in lower animals, is to promote flight.

Whenever, through an alarming perception, a system of energy paths in the brain, called the instinct of flight, is stimulated, the instinct is set in action. A series of impulses from the instinct immediately cause rapid movement on the part of certain groups of muscles, with consequent draining of nervous energy from other parts of the body. It is necessary that the active muscles should be given an extra supply of blood carrying more oxygen for increased combustion. Hence the heart and lungs increase their activity; as more blood goes to the muscles, the other parts of the body are deprived of their normally large supply.

It thus comes about that when the instinct of flight is stimulated, there follows rapid action of the heart, acceleration of breathing, paleness and coldness of the skin, a general shutting down of activity in those organs from which the blood is drained, with a dryness of the mouth and cessation of digestion. All of this is quite necessary when flight is indicated, but it often is embarrassing when applied to our civilized intercourse.

When typically activated by the instinct of flight, the muscles stimulate their respective internal sense organs with the result that the feeling of fear is experienced. According to the degree of stimulation of the instinct, there is activity of the viscera and muscles, and, as Professor James says, according to the degree of activity of the viscera and muscles, there is fear. The distressing feeling we have when fearful *is the result of stimulation of sense organs in the viscera and muscles.*

So it is that the alarming perception starts a circle of nervous excitement. Through motor nerves to the muscles, the instinct sends impulses which put the muscles in action. The activity of the muscles and viscera generate sensory impulses to the brain, producing the feeling we call emotion, and of course the emotion keeps on exciting the instinct. When a perception touches off the initial impulse, muscular contraction and emotion follow so simultaneously that it is difficult to realize that the perception is the primary but not the immediate cause of the emotion.

Emotional excitement continues to operate *until the desire which prompts it is satisfied,* exhaustion ensues, or the attention is diverted from the desire. The stimulation of the instinct of flight produces a desire to get away, and, even if we stand pat, our muscles are quite tense.

When emotion is marked, that is, when through violent contractions the muscles and viscera are sending in a large quota of impulses, the excitement only gradually dies out even after the cause is removed. For example, after the cause of great fear or anger is removed, it usually takes us several minutes before we regain complete composure, and *the more quickly we can relax our muscles, the sooner the fear or anger will leave us.*

In the fusion of sensation which makes up our entire feelings, varied and distinct physical elements—the psycho-physical processes—bring into play on stimulation a psychical whole, and we receive a general impression which depends for its character on both the elemental physical processes and the psychical atmosphere. In people suffering from "nerves," the initial disturbance lies not in the physical processes, but in the character of reaction to the psychical.

All sensations are either pleasant, indifferent, or unpleasant, and the general feeling they produce is called the *feeling tone of sensation.* On the physical side, the intensity, duration, and extensity of the stimulus all affect the character of the sensation, very strong stimuli nearly always being unpleasant. On the psychic side, however, no matter whether the stimulus be identically the same, the feeling effect will vary according to the control of the mind. Everybody will realize that identical stimuli are sometimes pleasant, sometimes the reverse, and sometimes neutral. The indifference point varies in different people, and in the same person at different times. The normal general feeling is mildly pleasant. Organic sensations which occur as the result of changes in the viscera have the most intense feeling tones, and most strongly determine appetite or aversion.

Such is the psycho-physical apparatus through which flows the current of life. On this most wonderful of instruments, the energy of the universe initiates a varied tune. Sometimes the senses sounded blend in a harmony of feeling that bespeaks pleasure and progress; and at other times a discord of sensation causes the animal to shrink and avoid the stimulus. Is it an accident that all living things are endowed with a tendency to prolong and repeat what is pleasant, and show aversion for pain? Will chemistry and mechanics elucidate why useful striving, pleasure, and progress go hand in hand? If science does aught, it points to the great uncomprehended truth of which scientific facts are the fragments. What a misfortune that they are often unused, and even abused, by those who need them to support the cause of peace, progress, and good-will toward men!

III

INSTINCTS, EMOTIONS, AND THE INTELLECT

THE sense organs are not only receivers of stimuli, but, in virtue of the feeling produced, are perceivers of stimuli. When an animal has its attention directed to an object, it is said to *perceive* that object. It is aware of the object through the feelings the object produces. In a vague way, it may " sense " other things and conditions in its environment, but there is one and only one focus to its attention. While the sensed objects which lie out on the margin of consciousness, might affect conduct in an indirect fashion, it is the concentrated and combined impulses that enter into a perception which regulate the animal's activities and determine its course.

We have seen that, when stimulated, sense organs send impulses which play upon psychophysical processes at the nerve centres and thereby produce sense impressions. It seems that such sense impressions, very much weakened, may be reproduced by impulses coming, not from sense organs, but from central cells in the brain. Such weak reproductions are called *memory images.*

The impulses from central cells reach the psycho-physical processes through *association nerve cells* which comprise countless numbers of nerve paths between central cells and the various sense areas of the brain. The junctions or synapses of the association cells, like other synapses or nerve centres, are resistant to the passage of impulses until they become organized with energy paths.

When an object is seen, the impulses which occasion the sense impression of the object tend to project themselves into association nerve paths which extend from the sensori-motor arcs to the central cells. If the impulses be sufficiently forcible or often repeated, they create energy paths through the synapses or nerve centres of the association cells. In this way a group of association cells become organized into a *perceptual system* of nerve paths the synapses of which have mutually low resistance. When any part of such a system is stimulated, the stimulus spreads immediately to all its parts. So it is that stimulation of a perceptual system will produce a memory image of the object which brought about the organization of the system.

In the brain as it develops, thousands of such perceptual systems representing objects in the environment, become organized. When impulses which promote perception reach the brain, they stimulate not only the psycho-physical processes of sensation, but one or more of the perceptual systems. Consequently there is a fusion of sensation and memory which enables one to recognize or perceive.

In man the vast majority of perceptual systems are the outcome of perceptions during his lifetime, and it is in virtue of the great wealth of association cells given to man that, as his experiences multiply, he is able to retain and accumulate perceptions, and to profit through them. In lower creatures association nerve cells form but a vestige of brain substance, and their perceptual systems, for the greater part, are inborn, and are not the outcome of a single lifetime's experience. It is only in higher animals like the dog or the ape that there is much evidence of knowledge being acquired during lifetime, and, in comparison to that of man, their knowledge is but a fragment.

All higher orders of creation have congenital perceptual systems or what might be described as inherited memory systems. With literally no education, the newly-hatched chick quite evidently recognizes that a grain of wheat is good food; and the young squirrel, even when brought up in seclusion, knows all about burying nuts for future advantage. These inborn perceptual systems are called *instincts*. The instinctive repugnance we feel toward snakes, or the tendency of a young horse to shy at any dark object on the road, bespeaks a vague inborn memory of ancestral experience.

Whenever an instinct is stimulated, a characteristic muscular response, called instinctive action, follows. Accompanying that action, and, as we have seen on account of it, there is generated by internal sense organs a feeling called *emotion*. *Instinctive action and emotion are two manifestations of the stimulation of an instinct.* Because to some extent we have the power of controlling our muscles when instinctive action naturally would accompany our emotions, we lose sight of the fact that, without the control, we should act just as an animal when our instincts are stimulated. Further, because we have not carefully observed the actions of animals, we are inclined to overlook the fact that they feel emotions as we do.

By watching another person's muscular actions, we can tell fairly accurately what feelings are accompanying those actions. Consider how a clever actor can depict emotion by the contortions of his face and the movements of his body. Also consider how when you walk along a dark street, and perceive something which stimulates the instinct of flight, if you control your muscular actions, the fear is moderate, but if you give full play to muscular action by breaking into a run, the fear is greatly aggravated.

Authorities differ with varying degrees of conservatism in their views of what comprises an instinct. Novelists, not to mention people in general, are exceedingly broad in their conception. Dr. William McDougall points out, however, that any nerve organization which on stimulation produces other than just one specific muscular response accompanied by one invariable type of feeling is to be ruled out of the classification. He recognizes in all higher animals eight primary instincts or nerve organizations, from which spring eight types of instinctive action and emotional feeling.

There is the instinct of flight, giving rise to the emotion of fear; the instinct of repulsion, with its emotion of disgust; the instinct of curiosity, and the emotion of wonder; the instinct of pugnacity, and the emotion of anger; the instincts of self-abasement (or subjection) and of self-assertion (or self-display), and the emotions of subjection and elation (or negative and positive self-feeling); and, finally, the parental instinct with the tender emotion Closely related to the parental, is the reproductive instinct. There are others of a less well defined emotional tendency, such as the gregarious or social instinct, and the instincts of acquisition and construction.

The stimulation of each of the instincts produces a typical desire, with muscular movement or tension apparent particularly in the muscles of the face. Emotion is desire. For example, anger is desire to dominate, wonder is desire to ascertain, and so on. The muscular movement accompanying emotion is a striving to satisfy the desire. Instinctive muscular action may appear very slight, as for example, simply a dilatation of the nostrils, or it may be exceedingly violent as in a fight to the death.

Instinctive action and emotion in animals under the stress of fear, anger, and disgust, are well recognized by everybody. Every experienced hunter has made use of the animal's instinct of curiosity to bag his game. The instinct of self-display or positive self-feeling is well manifested in the peacock, or in birds during the mating season. The blooded horse that arches his neck, lifts high his feet, and prances, when subjected to inspection, portrays the same emotion that in higher life largely constitutes pride. Self-abasement with its negative self-feeling, is illustrated in the slinking action of the little dog crawling on his belly with evident humility at the approach of a large and obviously important member of the canine family. The care with which some of the higher animals look after their young, and are even ready to die in their protection, points to the tender emotion as one of the strongest, and as the nucleus from which, in its higher development, springs all altruistic conduct.*

Like sensations, it is seldom that one elementary emotion is felt by itself. Usually several instincts are stimulated with varying intensity at one time, and the result is a blending of the emotional feel-

* For a full understanding of these important considerations, the reader is referred to "An Introduction to Social Psychology," by William McDougall (John W. Luce & Co.).

ings. While some emotions tend to be depressing and others elating, it is the intensity of the stimulus which determines the *emotional tone,* that is the pleasant or painful nature of the feeling.

In lower creatures the mechanism of the mind is like an automatic contrivance in a telephone system without a central operator. Every message which goes through is uncensored, allowed to go uncontrolled, and every message from outside compels action within. The currents which initiate fear, anger, wonder, and so on, compel actions of flight, combativeness, and curiosity, and it matters not at all whether the perception which turned on the current, actually was what it seemed to be, or whether the action which followed was warranted.

Such an automatic contrivance is the inheritance of the fish of the sea, the birds of the air, and the beasts of the jungle. It is the innate disposition born in every child, the bequest from ancestors who, for millions of years, have been the pioneers of personality.

When a babe is born, it comes into the world possessed of a brain mechanism which, although undeveloped, contains not only all the material parts given to the lower animals, but in addition, a vastly greater number of unorganized association nerve paths. At birth, but few of the millions of nerve paths throughout the body have been traversed by impulses. The instincts, however, have such low resistance to the passage of impulses that some of them are activated almost immediately, and instinctive action with emotion shows itself in the kicking and squalling occasioned by delivery into a cold and uncomfortable world.

In something like tens of seconds, instead of years, the babe repeats the steps of evolution in exactly the same order in which they occurred through the ages. By the time it is three years of age, the child has caught up to, and, in some respects, has passed the accomplishments of a fully developed lower animal. At this age the child's field of perception has become even wider than that of a mature animal, but in his limited field, the animal's perceptions are much more acute and accurate. The child, moreover, has acquired a much wider field of muscular action, being able to use its hands, tongue, and vocal organs much more effectively than the lower animal; but again, in its limited field, the animal quite outstrips the child in dexterity and strength of muscular action.

Little by little, as the mind of the child develops, it is enabled to perceive things never realized before. Gradually, for example, the pain of a pin prick, the sight of a pin and the sound of the word which the mother has pronounced become associated more and more stably in the child's mind, so that pain, or sight of pin, or sound of the word, recalls the other two factors in the association. This is not simply an association of ideas, but a coupling with a central cell of the perceptual sub-systems which have formed in the brain area of touch, in the area of sight, and in the area of sound. The connecting up takes place by reason of the perception, or the impulses which comprise it, over and over again travelling in unison to the same central cell. As the impulses, comprising perception, travel, they establish paths through the synapses or junctions of the association cells. That is to say, they organize the perceptual sub-systems into one larger system. The stimulation of the central cell will call to mind the associated memory images. Thus does memory become established.

Although we picture a thing in memory, it must not be supposed that memory images are all visual images. After sufficient experience, a child, born blind, can bring to mind the image of a musical tune, the image of the taste of butter-scotch taffy, the image of the pain of a pin prick, or the image of the perfume of a flower. His knowledge of these things cannot be complete, because the area of sight is left out of the web of association nerve paths, but his memory images, while less varied, are thought to be weakened reproductions of the actual sensations he experienced from these things in the remembered or forgotten past.

The instincts giving rise to the feelings we experience on perceiving any object or condition may establish energy paths between the instincts and the perceptual system representing the object. Should this occur, whenever the object is called to mind, the associated instincts with their feelings will be excited. About every object and condition of a person's environment, day by day, in ever-changing groups, there thus become organized feelings and ideas which are the result either of actual experience with such objects or of education about them. Such an organization of feeling about an object is a *sentiment.*

The sentiments always in the minds of people are like and dislike, or the stronger love and hate. The qualifications, however, we place on like and dislike, and the quantity of feeling we bestow, render our sentiments as variable as things themselves. We have sentiments not only about every individual, but about every object and condition with which we have had experience, personally, or through hearsay. We have sentiments about classes of people, and things in general, like Frenchmen, doctors, bungalows, horses, and so on, and we have sentiments about abstract things like truth, duty, self-control, and religion.

As the sentiment of love evolves, there develops in the brain an association of energy paths forming a web-like system which permits a stimulation of the emotions representative of love. The web is organized around the sub-system representing the object of affection, and connects with it the instincts which produce emotions of fear, anger, curiosity, subjection, elation, and, most prominently, tender emotion. For love to turn to hate, it is only necessary that the paths which permit the stimulation of elation and tender emotion should become dissociated, and be replaced by a path to the instinct of repulsion.

The character of our sentiments is one of the most important things about us, because, aside from the immediate impulse or stimulus from without, everything we do in life, and our attitude towards everything, is determined by our sentiments. Our sentiments, and those of other people, form what we might call our mental or spiritual environment. It is the most important part of our environment, and a part which enters into the environment of lower animals only in the most rudimentary way.

Whenever an impulse goes into a perceptual system, the feelings constituting the sentiment or belief which the system represents, are stimulated. These systems are open to continual change through new experience. The larger they grow, that is, the greater the number of other systems to which they become associated, the more powerful they become, and the more influence they exert over conduct. By suppression they may become forgotten and yet continue to exercise an important influence on the body. By disuse their paths may fade out and become extinct.

Everyone has noticed that when the energy of the brain is allowed to wander at random, it stimulates a series of memory images, one of which we say recalls another. For example, the image of white rose perfume recalls in sequence, a certain young lady, the theatre, a popular air, whistling at work, a hand laid on the shoulder, criticism, and so on indefinitely. It is no mere accident that these things appear in memory in this particular sequence. They do so because the perceptions were registered in sequence, and the perceptual systems are united by association paths. Just as a spider might pass from one web to another at the point where the two were connected with associating fibres, so the impulse which stimulates one system of nerve threads representing a memory, passes along the path of lowest resistance, and stimulates the next system most intimately associated.

Thoughts or ideas occur only because the sensory and emotional units which comprise them have been connected by energy paths through the force of some past perception. To be sure, the perceptual systems may be played upon, as a piano, giving rise to an infinite number of variations so that thought continually assumes a novel and original character. Thoughts are thus memories of past perceptions, coloured by feelings stimulated at the moment.

It is quite possible for the associated energy systems of the brain to be stimulated, and for impulses passing through them to activate the muscles and to produce emotional feeling, without our attention accompanying the activity. In other words, without perceiving them, we have thoughts which affect our conduct and produce feeling.

These are the so-called *subconscious thoughts* which normally play an important part in conserving conscious mental activity, and in some instances to too great a degree are permitted to take the place of conscious thinking and doing.

If all experiences remained fixed in the brain as perceptual or memory systems, there would be a great accumulation of unimportant detail, and a phenomenally large brain would be necessary. So it is that the normal function of *dissociation* prevails. This is brought about by a gradual increase in the resistance of synapses or nerve centres through which impulses have ceased to pass, so that the paths tend to fade out and with them the memory they represent. The function of dissociation also is to give the mind a rest, as in sleep, through temporarily rendering the energy paths of thought resistant to the passage of impulses. We shall consider later the abnormal manifestations of this function.

As the brain develops, it becomes more and more a storehouse for perceptual systems, which, on stimulation, produce memories of and feelings about experience. Such systems are the physical representatives of knowledge. The more accurate the perception which built the energy web, that is, the more truth that has gone into its organization, the more serviceable will be the memory of that perception. When new and varied experiences present themselves, the memories of past perception, whether true or false, are consulted in the archives of the brain, and dictate the conduct which follows. With a realization of the scientific theory that the observations of our daily life weave themselves into a material web, and that they become realities which comprise our capital stock for the future, more likely are we to pause and consider whether the material we are putting into our brains will make for future accuracy and happiness or inaccuracy and pain.

Day by day we all experience a multitude of sense impressions. The sense impressions may be compared to letters of the alphabet. As the letters of the alphabet form many and various words, so the sense impressions become associated to form sub-systems which represent various objects. As the words, in still greater variation, join to form sentences, so the sub-systems combine into systems which are analogous to ideas and memories of experience. Under the influences of sensation, emotion, and sentiment, these associate to compose a thesis of life.

Let us now consider the mechanism of the mind in action. Mrs. Vanity Fair comes to call, and the fleeting feelings which her presence excites are sensations with either pure emotions and tendencies, or more likely, some combination of them. Feeling a little pleasurable excitement, we gaze at her Parisian gown with wonder plus a little negative self-feeling. Such a combination of emotions would comprise admiration. If Mrs. Vanity Fair added a tinge of fear to our admiration, our feeling would be one of awe. On the other hand, if by speaking kindly of the children, the visitor aroused our tenderness, and it was coupled with the emotion of subjection or negative self-feeling, we should experience a feeling of gratitude. Through combinations of two or more emotions being stimulated in unison, we might go on to feel all grades of scorn, contempt, envy, bashfulness, and so on.

While these feelings might readily change from moment to moment, as our knowledge of Mrs. Vanity Fair increased, there would gradually become organized in connection with her, a more stable feeling, a feeling that would come to mind every time we heard her name. This feeling would, of course, be a sentiment. Suppose that our sentiment about her might be summed up by saying that we liked her, but considered her a snob. In time our sentiment might be composed of feelings of a very different nature. In any event, although we might not think so, our sentiment regarding Mrs. Vanity Fair would have a greater effect on our own bodies than on her.

Our sentiment about Mrs. Vanity Fair having budded and grown, should we meet her, we should be very likely to have other feelings which are dependent on a sentiment, and in time may help to mould it. For example, if in addition to liking Mrs. Vanity Fair, she aroused our anger with her snobbishness, we should have a feeling of reproach. If, in addition to this, she incurred our sympathy, our feeling would be one of anxiety. Again, if to our tender emotion, there were added anger, positive self-feeling, and desire of acquisition, we should experience jealousy. Other combinations of passing emotion with a more or less fixed sentiment, might cause feelings of revenge, resentment, and shame.

If Mrs. Vanity Fair impressed us with her strength of character, we should probably entertain towards her a sentiment of respect. In the sentiment of respect there is little of tender emotion, and a considerable amount of elation and subjection, or positive and negative self-feeling. Respect centers about all sorts of things and people, but in no relation is the sentiment as important as in regard for the self. Our happiness, our usefulness, and our satisfaction in life, in great measure are dependent on the strength of our sentiment of self-regard.

IV

THE MORAL SELF

AT the time of the origin of life, living things did not act on their own account, but their movements were purely reflex action. Under such circumstances, feeling could not have been the cause of action, and pleasure could not have been the inspiration of striving. In time, however, pleasure was derived from actions which, as a class, were true or well-adapted, and pain from harmful actions, so that the living thing tended to repeat and to become more proficient in what was pleasant and serviceable, and to avoid what was painful. Pleasure and pain have thus assumed a somewhat reversed position, so that they now appear to be both the cause and the effect of behaviour or conduct.

Just as throughout the ages, all life, whatever its environment, has striven to achieve whatever gives pleasure, and to avoid whatever causes pain, so the child comes into the world with a strong innate tendency to seek and strive after those things which produce pleasant sensations—those things which bring comfort and pleasure to the body. From this fact some good people would have us draw the inference that the child is " born in sin." This is to argue that all animals are sinning when, in animal fashion, they seek bodily pleasure and avoid pain.

The fact is that those animals which are successful in finding the maximum of bodily pleasure and comfort are the finest specimens in the animal kingdom. Just what constitutes the maximum of bodily pleasure is a matter for further consideration. It is obvious, however, that in animals, successful striving, bodily pleasure, and satisfaction are God-given identities. Man's striving secures a higher reward in happiness, and his life is sadly lacking in satisfaction when he achieves only bodily pleasure and comfort.

During the first years of its life, except for its potentialities, a child in every respect is simply a little animal. It does not develop beyond the animal stage until it has covered the steps of evolution, and has acquired in its brain perceptual systems representative of intellect.

With the addition of energy paths which afford thought and sentiment, there develops a higher type of feeling tone which is experienced but little by the lower animal—a feeling tone of joy or sorrow. While in a way closely related to bodily pleasure and pain, joy and sorrow are largely dependent on mental associations and association systems in the brain, and therefore are largely man's monopoly.

With the addition of joy and sorrow, man's striving no longer confines itself to an effort to gratify bodily appetite, and to attain the pleasure of the senses, but it expresses itself in a striving to reach the ideals of his intellect. In other words a new self—an intellectual self—gradually becomes added to his prehistoric animal self. A new set of desires born of sentiment become added to the innate animal desires. Too often the desires of the animal self are out of accord with those of the intellectual self, and the two selves act at cross purposes.

It will be recalled that impulses travel more readily along nerve paths which from the standpoint of evolution are the oldest. All the innate systems, like instincts, in fact, all the nerve cell combinations with which we are born, offer but little resistance to impulses, and, without any effort on our part, impulses soon make a way through them, and give rise to various shades of sensation and emotional feeling. Such feeling is purely innate, and differs but slightly from the feeling of animals.

Many people regard feeling or emotional display as something that denotes strength of character. The fact is that in the matter of pure feeling, or emotion without the use of intelligence, the lower animal can present a finer exhibition than man. Undoubtedly the individual with a wealth of emotional energy has a gift which may prove of great advantage, but it may prove even a greater disadvantage. This depends on how the feelings are regulated.

The lower animal makes little attempt to regulate

its feelings. It has not the wherewithal to do so. On the other hand, at birth, the babe inherits a potential power which is given only to man—a power which places him in dominion over all that is lower in the scale of evolution, a power which may be developed or may lie dormant—the power of the moral self.

In lower creatures, and in man until the self comes into play, all action is blind obedience to forces other than intellectual. It is pure re-action. The ancient dynasty of the brain consists of an hierarchy of rulers, each of whom not only at one stage of evolution held supreme command, but still lives, and seeks to rule. The intellect is the latest claimant to the throne, and is a usurper of very limited power. Unless the intellect has the support of the moral self, its barbarous predecessors will arise in their might, and bedevil its ideals, pollute its wishes, and establish confusion by permitting the alternate sway of contending factions.

Without the moral self we should be but marionettes which, to the stimulus of outside forces, dance on the stage of life, are driven hither and thither, and take no part in the shaping of destiny. As the self asserts itself, the more are we able to choose a line of action independent of, or even in opposition to, outside forces; the more are we at liberty to exercise free will; the more do we enjoy freedom. As the self develops, the more is the intellect made the governor of action, and the more content become the subservient forces in the brain to carry out the duties of their own sphere.

Volumes have been written on the character of the great force which comprises the moral self, and while, in this place, it could serve no good purpose to go into a lengthy discussion of the matter, it nevertheless will be well for you to grasp the reality of the self, and not to regard it simply as a vague influence which, in some incomprehensible way, has a most important effect on men's lives.

We have seen that in all living things, at every waking moment, outside forces are sending impulses to the nerve centres, and impelling the muscles to act. The moral self in varying degree possesses the marvellous faculty of being able to gather up these impulses from the nerve paths of the brain, and, in spite of resistance, to direct them along the paths it would have them go. Not only this, but more marvellous still, in its higher development, the self is able to hold in check, and even discharge impulses which, in a lower animal, would spend themselves in muscular action. The first function or purpose of the moral self is called *volition,* and the second, *control.*

To revert to our analogy of the telephone system: in the lower animal the system is automatic; every message or impulse, as we have seen, goes on to the muscles without interruption, and muscular action is inevitable. In man, a central operator or self presides over the system, and, to varying degrees in different individuals, takes over the management of the nervous switchboard. As the central operator develops power, more and more can he direct which messages will be given the right of way over others, and which will be held up or censored. A very important part of his work is the filing of records in the brain. On the pains the self takes to obtain true perceptions, and on the system adopted in filing these, will depend most of the body's welfare or misfortune.

In the doing of things about us, two courses are open. We can allow ourselves to be quite effortless, and take cognizance only of those things which force themselves upon our attention, or which give us pleasure to carry out. This is the half conscious fashion—the line of least resistance—the existing by reaction. In the alternative course, we force ourselves to be wide-awake. We have the determination to get the full value out of living and doing—to perceive everything we see, hear, taste, and so on—to find the full meaning of it, and to store it in our memory as something for future use. This is living, this is using the perception God has given us, this is developing personal power.

People do not travel very far upon the road of life before they come to a keen realization that all things are not what they seem, that into the most commonplace things there generally enters an element of deception, causing an ever variable combination of truth with untruth. One great function of the moral self when the intellect perceives a truth, is to have the body make use of it, and when the intellect perceives what is false, to protect the body from it. The distinguishing of true from false is not accomplished by sizing up a thing on the feeling it produces, because quite possibly what is false may produce feelings identical with those produced by what is true. Rather do we have to concentrate the wandering energy of the brain on the thing perceived, refer to like things stored in our memory, and, through comparison of the present experience with the past, determine the actual truth. This process is called reasoning.

While a line of clever ancestors may render us predisposed to develop good reasoning faculties, the perceptual systems which make for reasoning ability have to be built up in their entirety after birth. Reasoning ability is therefore largely dependent on mental effort or volition. Furthermore, the reasoning material is wholly the result of either personal perception, or the acceptance of the experience of other people, which last is called education.

As our experiences in life increase, as our perceptions become more and more acute, we will observe that certain results inevitably follow certain happenings. We will associate cause with effect, and so establish a basis for reasoning. Reasoning is the ability to find the old in the new. The fuller our stores of knowledge of fact, the richer will become our perceptions, and the more general in their application will we find certain rules and principles.

Finally there comes a time when the majority of new experiences and things are without difficulty assigned their right classification, and are understood by the properties they have in common with experiences that have passed, or things which are understood. The more accurate our perceptions, or the more we make a habit of taking the trouble to attribute the correct cause to certain effects, and vice versa, the better will be the reasoning power. On the cultivation of this habit of being particular with regard to the truth in a perception, hangs much of the future happiness in life.

Reasoning or making use of our intellects, requires effort; it is the work of our moral selves. It is so much more comfortable not to be bothered, just to let ourselves take a vacation, and to get along on the feeling of the thing. It is much easier to let the impulses travel willy-nilly through the well-worn nerve paths of early evolution; it is much easier to use the primeval animal part of ourselves; it requires no effort to let the moral self shrivel. But if at all we value our human heritage, if we would rise above and have dominion over the beast, we must day by day—not spasmodically, but each day and every day—add a little to the power of self through concentrating, and forcing the energy of the brain across the synapses or nerve centres of nerve paths postnatal in origin.

Our habits in life develop so gradually that it is difficult for us to realize that the commonplace everyday things we do, ever required a degree of effort beyond that of the present. Yet, if we pursue careful retrospection, or better still, if we watch the development of a child, we can see that each advancement is gained only through painstaking effort, that each repetition of an act diminishes the effort necessary for its accomplishment, and that finally the action becomes automatic, that is, may be left to carry itself out without any volition whatever.

Take, for example, the matter of piano-playing: with what concentrated effort does the child regulate the muscles of his hands and arms before he learns to play a scale! Or again, what months of effort, failure, and trying again, before the speaking of a simple sentence in a foreign language has become an accomplishment! Just as long as advancement is to continue, just as long as something new is to be accomplished, the moral self must exercise its function of volition, must assemble or concentrate the energy of the brain, and force it along paths which otherwise would lie dormant or even non-existent.

Just as from lack of exercise, the muscles of an arm become flabby, and quite incapable of doing work when occasion requires, so the moral self loses strength through not exercising volition. Conversely, the greater the daily effort the self makes, the stronger becomes its power of volition. This matter of making effort, of concentration, of overcoming obstacles, is, like everything else, largely a matter of habit. The more we make effort in our daily work, the easier it becomes for us to do so. The more we funk, the harder it becomes to make effort when we wish to do so.

Every happening recurs more readily in the old than in a new way. In other words, everything tends to develop a habit, and becomes changed as a result of the habit. For example, a paper is folded more easily the second time than the first; as water trickles more easily along a surface where once it has found a path. In the same way, the process of putting impulses across resistant synapses or nerve centres in nerve paths, becomes less difficult with each successful attempt, until finally, left to themselves, the impulses will take the course they have been trained by the moral self to follow.

As day by day the moral self forces the energy of life through new nerve paths, the demand for new cells brings development. Every accomplishment thus is represented by nerve cells and energy paths through their junctions, and the power of the self in one direction stands in arithmetical proportion to the number of paths, and the depth to which they are worn.

The great majority of people are fairly well developed in the matter of volition. This function of the moral self is put into practice daily through the school life of the child, and usually by the time a man is ready to take his part in the world, he has learned to a fair extent the art of overcoming resistance. Unfortunately, the second great function of the self, namely control, is left to the care of people who, too often, have neither developed it themselves, nor have the right idea of how to teach it to another.

While it is of inestimable importance that we all should learn to put impulses across in spite of resistance, it is of even greater importance to our welfare and to the safety of others that we should learn to control impulses which, if allowed to go into action, would be harmful to us or to the community at large. Until self-control has become automatic, it is easier to be an animal than a man, because the innate desires cry out for satisfaction, and would have us deny the rights of others through gratification of our animal selves.

Self-control is not volition, is not effort. It differs from volition as the process of subtraction differs from addition, or as letting go differs from holding on. The vast majority of people seek self-control through effort, and this is why too often they fail. For example, a strong impulse comes to do a thing which obviously is unwise. The individual says—" I wish to do this thing, but I shall control myself." Too often, not understanding just how the impulse should be controlled, the moral self allows it to go through to the muscles, but sends at the next moment another impulse to opposing groups of muscles.

These are tactics we should despise in a diplomat! The result is that the opposing groups of muscles stand out taut, each pulling against the other. While undoubtedly some overt act is held in check, good energy is wasted. The body as a whole is deprived of strength with nothing to show for it, and the individual congratulates himself on his fine self-control, but wonders why his body is so tired!

If an impulse is to be controlled, if central operator is to censor a message successfully, that impulse or message has to be put out of business. The moral self has to kill it. Otherwise it will wait until the control is not quite so vigilant, when it will steal across into action. How often, some time later, we do the very thing we said we would not do, and wonder how it happened! But how kill the impulse? *By giving up the desire.* To say we will not do a thing, and to go on wishing to do it, is childish, because undoubtedly the desire sooner or later will get its way.

A mental state of perfect willingness to forego the desire must replace the "I want." Then and only then we have true self-control. Self-control is thus the disciplining of the wish—the dominance of the moral self over desire—the bestowing of the energy which comprises the censored impulse, on other activities. This is the second great function of the moral self which taxes even the strongest personalities. There is one word which describes it better than all others, and that word is *renunciation.* The renunciation of desire when, in the discrimination of the intellect, the desire is unwise, is the finest faculty of the mind, and the far too little appreciated explanation of self-control.

Like volition, self-control has to be built up with ceaseless watchfulness and repeated endeavour. It is an art, the foundations of which must be laid day by day. If the child and the student were made to bestow as much pains on the study of self-control as on mathematics, what money would be saved on prisons and asylums! If the effort of all religious institutions were directed more toward developing the function of the moral self and tolerance to the growing and healthy tendency to question all suggestion, how much more far reaching, how much more powerful a part the Church would play!

V

ENVIRONMENT AND ADAPTATION

EVERYTHING in the world from a microbe to a mountain is in process of constant change, advantageous to evolution or progress. The statement is difficult to accept, because all about us we see things which are destructive and hurtful, things which *appear* to be doing anything but working to the advantage of the universe. On reflection it will be realized, however, that these things are hurtful only to man's selfish wishes, and not to the interests of evolution.

In order that there may be evolution, it is necessary that when things cease to co-operate as they are they should be reduced to elements which, being re-united in some other form, will be serviceable to progress. The things men regard as vile, are, in fact, things in a process of reduction or disintegration. Whatever a thing may have become, each elementary constituent in itself is pure and good, and presently will combine with other elements in a reorganization, the usefulness and beneficence of which men will more readily recognize. Furthermore, a thing may *appear* evil to man, because its function is to disintegrate that which has ceased to progress, and which therefore must be scrapped and used in other fields of activity. To us the effects of disintegration are much more apparent than the cause, but, although we may not perceive it, there always is a cause, namely *failure tc progress.* The forces of evolution will not tolerate inertia, notwithstanding that time seems to be but a small consideration:

> "Though the mills of God grind slowly,
> Yet they grind exceeding small."

So it is that all energy travels in a circle, and has the appearance of moving in contrary directions, but all the while is working towards the one end. In one half of the circle, which may be called the negative, energy tends to pull down, disintegrate, reduce to elements. In common parlance we use the word destroy, and the thought accompanying the word is that when a thing is destroyed it is rendered extinct. This is but one of the many illusions of life. It is a scientific fact that nothing can be rendered extinct. It can be completely altered, disintegrated into its elements or electrons, but not nullified. For example, we burn a piece of wood, and, gazing at the little pile of gray ash, we tell ourselves the wood is destroyed. Did we but collect the smoke carbon, the gases, and the ash, or their primary ingredients, we should find, by actual measurement, a sum total equal to the original. In the same way, it is impossible to destroy energy—the energy of life, psychic energy, or any other kind. It may be changed from one character to another, but the sum total remains constant.

Energy travels with even greater flow in the positive direction than in the negative, and the excess of positive over negative forms a margin which is progress, or evolution. The positive energy is the building up or integrating process, which is in keeping with our own wise wishes and satisfaction in life. It is quite obvious that the *sine qua non* of our existence is progress or building up. Everything points to the fact that we are agents entrusted with a great deal of energy to be expended in the interests of evolution.

Without the negative force—the energy which reduces things to their elements—there would be no striving toward adaptation on the part of living things, no desire to conform to what is progressive, and consequently no stimulus or necessity to progress and no evolution to higher forms. Disintegrating energy plays quite as important a part in making living things strive to adapt themselves to their environment, as does the reward in satisfaction which comes from adaptation. Necessity not only is the mother of invention, it is the mother of all striving and progress. Not only are we coaxed forward with rewards of pleasure and happiness, we are driven forward from necessity.

Without entering into a prolonged philosophical

discussion, it will be recognized that what men call *truth* is intimately wrapped up in the onward sweep of evolution; that truth is that which harmonizes with universal progress, and that untruth is the disintegrating factor in men's lives.

In scant detail we have followed evolution from the time that life embodied itself in matter, and we have observed the steady increase of power each eon of time has conferred on all life which has adapted itself to the demands of nature. In greater or less measure, each million of years has brought its higher order. In the comparatively short period of time covered by history, we recognize between the caveman and the finer types of civilization, a gain in personal power, stupendous as it is significant. In the last century alone, the inventions which assist adaptation, and the discoveries, or in other words, the uncoverings of truth, which help to avoid suffering, cause us to regard the future with awe, and to wonder whither away it all leads.

Although no man or institution is able to fathom the whole mystery of truth, two great classes of experience have throughout time served as guides to all living things. On the one hand, pain and sorrow are indicative of untrue conduct or misadaptation; on the other, pleasure and happiness accompany or follow true conduct or adaptation. Suffering may be the result of untrue conduct on the part of others, and likewise, benefit may accrue through another's true conduct or adaptation.

Moreover, cause and effect may be so far removed that they remain unrecognized.

The environment of the lower animal is small in comparison to that of man. The things to which the animal is required to adapt itself are only the material things, but failure in adaptation is fraught with suffering, and more or less prompt extermination. The animal not only must strive to adapt itself, but must make a success in its striving or lose its life.

Consider, for example, an animal overtaken by a blizzard. It either adapts itself to the condition by digging a hole in the earth, and so fortifies itself against the cold, or it assumes a "can't-be-bothered" attitude, and fails to obey the prompting of instinct. In the first instance, it undoubtedly has to exert itself; in so doing it is rewarded by the pleasure of comfort and avoidance of suffering. When the blizzard is over, it emerges fit in body, and not only strengthened by its exercise, but able, perchance, to make a meal out of some animal which is too cold either to fight or to run. The animal that finds it too great an effort to follow the dictate of its instincts, fails in adapting itself to the storm, and compromises by standing in the shelter of a bush, not only experiences suffering, but frequently so reduces its powers of resistance that, later, it falls a prey to the animal which takes the trouble to adapt itself. Of course, such consequences are not immediately inevitable; sooner or later, however, in the struggle for existence, the animal which fails to strive, and so fails at adaptation, loses its life.

Ornithologists tell us that every year, when the time comes for the birds to migrate to a warmer climate, there are always some birds which are left behind. Whether or not they have developed any nervous inability to act has not been determined. There is no doubt, however, that for their failure to conform to what they doubtless feel is right, they forfeit their privilege of living. In this way only the strivers are perpetuated. The misfits and failures return their lives to that sum of energy which always was, and is, and is to be. The animal which strives, not only finds the finest living conditions, and is rewarded with the healthiest and most fitly developed body, but his pleasures in life are proportionate to his successful adaptation.

We may well imagine that the "soft snap" or the elysium of idleness, could never become an ideal in the jungle! Neither would there be room for an ideal of over-indulgence. The animal which gives way to excessive gratification of its appetites, incapacitates itself to cope with its environment. What a bore to have always to act wisely or lose one's life; and what an insult to the animal kingdom to call a drunken man a beast!

How misplaced are our ideals of pleasure and pain that we should point to the jungle and shudder! Pleasure accompanies and is the result of successful adaptation. Unsuccessful adaptation being short-lived in the jungle, it follows that, with the beast, there is little opportunity for depressed emotional states. The pleasure of successful striving is thus so forced upon the animal, that, in its limited capacity, the animal's percentage of pleasure over pain far surpasses our own.

An animal's environment is made up entirely of material things; an animal's striving is limited to the attainment of material things, and so the possibility of enjoyment in an animal's life is limited to *pleasure,* and the extreme of suffering is limited to the bodily pain of death. Whether or not pleasure and pain are the chief *causes* of the animal's striving is beside the point. The fact is that pleasure inevitably accompanies successful striving or adaptation to the material environment, and pain or death just as inevitably goes hand in hand with lack of effort or indifference.

With the advance to civilization, two great changes have come about. Man enjoys comparative immunity against more or less prompt extermination for failure to adapt himself to his environment. The results of his misadaptation are not so dramatically evident. At the same time, his capacity for suffering and mental anguish too often makes him realize that there are some states worse than death. The second great difference is that into the environment of man, as distinct from that of lower animals, there enter thoughts and sentiments, and the multitude of mental or spiritual influences which emanate from these.

From early childhood to the grave, by storing in our brains the memory of our own experiences and the experiences of others as gathered in general knowledge, we acquire gradually a new environment. To the moderately educated person, a time arrives when his store of memories, with the thoughts they bring on stimulation, occupies a greater part of his environment than do material things. It is well if our memories and thoughts are of such a character that we can dwell in harmony with them. Then there are the expressed thoughts and ideas of other people. What a lifelong struggle, what continuous striving to adapt ourselves to them—not criticisms, censure, and unjust ridicule only, but more pernicious, flattery, that "praise undeserved" which "is scandal in disguise!"

Adaptation to our physical environment is largely the work of our bodies. If we would have the material necessities of life, we must till the soil, manufacture commodities, and construct towns and cities. By successful striving with our bodies, we secure comfort and pleasure. On the other hand, adaptation to our mental environment, our realm of thought, sentiment and wish, is the work of the intellect and the moral self. In proportion to the success of our striving for adaption in this respect, we secure *happiness.*

Many people think that satisfaction and happiness emanate from the material part of their environment, the part which includes fine houses, pretty clothes, good food, and so on. In our environment, materials of every kind, even if beautifully manufactured and finely finished, stand in the same relation to us as the materials which comprise the environment of lower animals, stand in relation to them. Conversely, just as material things in our environment afford us physical satisfaction, bodily comfort, and sensuous pleasures, so well-constructed dug-outs, luscious herbage, and fine fur, give to the animal a well-nourished body, and afford it pleasure.

To us, as to animals, material things afford a multitude of pleasures, but the wealth of the Indies or the luxury of princes cannot give us happiness. How many people make the mistake of supposing that happiness is composed of a sum of pleasures! Happiness is no such thing. It is a common experience to have pleasures thrust upon us when we are utterly unhappy, and, perhaps less common, to hold our happiness through all, whilst experiencing pain and distress.

To a limited extent, the material things of life are necessary, undoubtedly, if for nothing else than to meet the body's physical needs; beyond this, however, they are quite superfluous to heights of happiness which few comprehend, let alone experience. Far from being an essential to happiness, the surfeit of material gain, acquired with but little or no volition, is responsible more than aught else for the suffering soul which distorts the face of pleasure.

We have seen that all things work together for the good, not of man, but of the universe as a whole, and that where there is lack of progress there is a wearing down process that gradually eliminates the parts which fail to co-operate. Human beings, like cells in the body, are units within the universe. Like the cells of the body, they cannot live to themselves alone; they must co-operate and adapt themselves to each other, or they will be worn away.

When we fail to adapt ourselves to our environment of thought, and there is friction, it is obvious that we, or the source of the friction, or both, must become changed if adaptation is to come about. Either the source of friction in the environment has to be changed to suit or co-operate with us, or our mental attitudes have to be changed to co-operate with spiritual conditions in the environment. In other words, where there is resistance, either the environment or we have to become changed.

Darwin has shown how, in animal life, very considerable bodily changes have taken place in order that animals might adapt themselves to inexorable physical environments. This gives us an important cue with regard to our spiritual environments. In the realm of thought, there are conditions which are inevitable. It is a foregone conclusion that into each human life there must enter thoughts which are sordid, words which are cutting, ideas which are false, betrayals of trust, calumnies, slanders, flatteries, and misrepresentations. These are but comparable to reefs, quicksands, pitfalls, frost, and fire in the material world, and as such should not occasion the surprise, the indignation, and vehemence of feeling which we repeatedly manifest at their occurrence. Some mental trials like some pitfalls and quicksands in nature, can be changed and rendered less formidable, but the great majority occur with the regularity of frost and fire, and if we do not with a cloak of indifference or by following common sense, adapt ourselves to them, our souls will suffer ceaselessly.

Instead of spending our lives in weary and fruitless striving to change our spiritual environments, or in running away from what is unpleasant, we should concentrate our energies in an unremitting effort so to alter the attitude of our own minds that we may live in harmony with, and derive the good (for always there is *some* good) from even the things we most dislike. By far the greatest harm from another's untrue conduct arises through the attention we give to it. If we would make it a rule always to ride roughshod over feeling in ourselves, and hold our attention solely to what is upbuilding, we should soon find happiness. Through daily effort of the moral self, we are brought finally to realize that even in ribald thoughts and ungenerous taunts, there lies a challenge to the self to fulfil its function, through bringing about perfect adaption of the mind to its spiritual environment.

Happiness and satisfaction in life can come in no way other than through successful striving of the moral self to adapt the body and the mind to their physical and mental environment. Without one paramount principle to guide it in the accomplishment of this work, the self would be doomed to failure. We have now to consider that great principle, the application of which will make for adaptation and personal power.

VI

THE CRITERION OF GOOD AND EVIL

WE have seen that wrapped up in every emotion is a desire, and that the stronger the desire, the more intense is the emotion. Sometimes one's desires are unconscious, but often they assume the form of conscious wishes. We all have wishes which may with advantage be fulfilled, and wishes which fortunately are doomed to failure; wishes for what is wise, and wishes for what is selfish; wishes that die a natural death, and wishes which would dominate the soul; wishes of which we are proud, and wishes which surreptitiously cause us to blush with shame. Our conscious wishes are but the buoys which float on the stream of striving, and show us whither away our energy would carry us. It is well if our moral self sits at the helm, and adapts the course of the craft to the erratic currents which sweep us too often from our bearings, and strand us on the shoals of irritability and despair.

If we make it our object in life to satisfy all our wishes, or even the majority of them without discrimination, we shall inevitably subject ourselves to the disintegrating forces of nature. Unless the moral self takes the energy which, if left to itself, would continually stimulate the wrong sort of feelings, and uses it to further those wishes which work for adaptation of mind and body, one wish will pull down while the other builds up, and discouragement will be inevitable.

Our position is practically this—we find ourselves launched in a world of material and spiritual things on which to apply our energy of life. We can use this energy to build up or to pull down; we can invest it wisely and increase our capital, or we can dissipate it and decrease our capital. We can fail to use it, and in time it will reduce us to our elements. There is only one thing it is impossible to do, and that is to remain inert. *We must progress or lose that which we have.*

Through interfering with our wishes, this scheme of things may appear to us as most inconsiderate, but that is only because we regard ourselves with an importance which is quite misplaced. Once we can expand sufficiently to obtain the hint of a million years' perspective, we shall be able to realize just what personal objections can amount to, in the face of the onward sweep of evolution. If we be dissatisfied with things as they are, the great negative force of life will, without any exertion on our part, reduce us gradually to elements which, sooner or later, will be used for the purpose which occasioned us too great an effort.

One fact stands out clearly: without the struggle for existence through millions of years, and the daily weeding out of the faulty and unfit, man could never have realized that fragment of God in himself, his own soul. Without the pain which inevitably accompanies or follows every false move or deviation from truth, every sin of *omission* as well as of commission, what reason would there be to strive? Without the pleasures, the joys, and the happiness which just as inevitably accompany or follow service and successful adaptation, what would mere existence hold? How childish to criticize the universal scheme of things for consequences which, since the beginning of life, inevitably have followed lack of effort and indifference to truth!

Most of us realize that the reducing process is synonymous with bodily pain and mental torture, and that the building-up process brings unbounded joy and gladness. Some of us, on scientific reasoning, further believe that the balanced building and development of our highest mental and spiritual processes, establish an integration of spiritual force which persists as an entity, after the body is reduced to its elements. As Matthew Arnold so beautifully expresses it in " Immortality ":

> ". . . the energy of life may be
> Kept on after the grave, but not begun;
> And he who flagg'd not in the earthly strife,
> From strength to strength advancing—only he,
> His soul well knit, and all his battles won,
> Mounts, and that hardly, to eternal life."

Suppose, however, that you accept your life simply on the prose basis of actual experience; even so, it is to the bodily and spiritual interest of mortal man, not only to strive and build with temperate might, but carefully to consider the character of those wishes which, when gratified, inevitably bring the negative force into play.

It matters little how men classify conduct, the true criterion of good or evil is an inward sense of happiness or of suffering. Our real goodness is proportional to the amount we build up. Our evil is relative to the extent to which we retard direct progress. Goodness lies not in believing, but in doing. Undoubtedly believing is an important fundamental to doing, but there is no virtue in any belief by itself. The virtue lies only in the progress which the belief stimulates. The value of a belief is not to be estimated by the people who entertain it, but by the fruits of their lives.

As illustrated in the humble home of the peasant, satisfaction in life is much greater with simple beliefs which are lived up to and with a little knowledge that is applied, than with a great deal of learning which plays but a small part in influencing conduct. That the justice of nature exceeds human justice is wonderfully illustrated by the fact that nature requires more of the man who knows than of the one who is ignorant, and increases punishment to him who consciously or sub-consciously realizes more adequately the error of his ways.

Exquisite are the joys of refinement, and rapturous the fruits of learning, but a realization that our knowledge of truth is not applied, is a source of constant discontent.

With our practice of enforcing intellectual training and of leaving psychic or moral development to what is often no more than haphazard influence, it is not unnatural that the two forms of development, intellectual and psychic, prove, in many cases, unequal in the race. Thus in one and the same individual we sometimes find the intellect of a man and the moral self of a child. Such individuals although intellectual, are not wise.

Wisdom is a double quality virtue—the product of knowledge of truth carried out in action. We may be told a truth over and over again, and we may believe it, but unless we have applied it, and, through experience, have made it a part of ourselves, we are not wise with regard to that truth. By itself, knowledge is but an artificial reproduction of the wisdom of others. Anyone with sufficient memory can be a parrot, but words of genuine wisdom come only from the balanced brain, where knowledge of truth has been applied in conduct, and the individual speaks from personal experience.

The distinction which, too long, has been made between goodness and wisdom, is, from a health standpoint and for practical purposes, as imaginary as it is unreasonable. Where in the world of goodness can one find anything which is unwise; where in the world of wisdom, anything which is bad? What is the advantage, other than authority's misplaced indifference, in being " only unwise, but not bad " ? If an act be unwise, it causes disintegration; if it be bad, it entails the same thing. Although we may seek shelter under a false classification of conduct, the fact is that the suffering which results from being " unwise " or " bad " is proportionate not to what the conduct is termed, but to the degree of its interference with the purpose of existence.

Likewise the reward of virtue, whether it be designated wisdom or goodness, is proportionate to the service rendered the universe. Let us away with distinctions which, too long, have confused the issue. Let us lay the whole stress on wisdom, and drop from our discussion the word goodness, which for obvious reasons has fallen into disrepute.

Distinctions, also, which have been made between various forms of evil, are artificial and confusing. If our object be to eliminate pain and suffering, and to promote health and happiness, our vision must be cleared of the dust of moral inconsistencies and of all qualifications of virtue and evil, which owe their origin so largely to interests of class and privilege. We must lay stress on things as they actually are, and not on things as a pleasure loving public, or particular institutions, find it convenient to regard them.

Some people are not entirely convinced that under every circumstance it is to their advantage to act in accord with what they know to be true. They believe that they can get ahead of nature and derive selfish benefit through conduct which is disintegrating. They undoubtedly have failed to realize that nothing which impedes the general good of living things can redound ultimately to individual advantage. They have lost sight of the fact that evil is synonymous with disintegration or interference with direct progress, whether it be our own, or another's, or that of the world at large.

In the erroneous belief that the self can benefit at the expense of truth lies every unmoral and immoral act known to society, that is, every antisocial act. Murder, theft, adultery, intemperance, indolence, flattery, what you will, each and all have their origin in mistaken selfishness, in the unfortunate supposition that the self can benefit from something which is unwise. The cheerfulness with which people say, " I know it is unwise, but I am going to do it," is conclusive evidence of failure to realize the very basis of morality, namely, that *knowingly to act unwisely is to enfeeble the moral self, and to subject the body to inevitable punishment.*

Of the multitude of unwise acts in life, the laws of man lay the greater stress and punishment on the sins of commission or misplaced activities;

nature causes the greater suffering for the sins of omission or of indolence. We are not interested at present especially in the laws of man, except in so far as they have lost sight of the meaning of evolution. Our chief interest centers in natural laws, and on responsibility, not to man, but with reference to nature.

If we follow the law of nature, that is, the one law of truth, we shall not offend nature and can allow all other law to take care of itself. This simplifies things very much, because there is in nature only one wrong and one right, and punishment or reward is proportional to the *degree* to which we fail or succeed in striving for the right. The one *wrong* is *selfishness,* which might better have been called mistaken selfishness. The one *right* is that we shall make our bodies and mental attitudes *conform to what we realize is wise.*

Selfishness is bound up intimately with our wishes. We continually feel we should like to do things which our intellect considers unwise; conversely, our reason often says, "it is wise to do this thing," and our wish answers, "too much bother." A conflict ensues between the moral self and the unwise wish. If the moral self be downed, of course it loses power, and on the next occasion is less capable of holding its own. The moral self may be downed so often that finally, in some act, a degree of selfishness may be reached which is utterly surprising to the person himself.

"To think these hands could work such madness
here—
This envious head devise this misery!"

Fear of social ostracism may compel the moral self to exercise a limited control, at least within the laws of man. Under such circumstances, one's wishes and the moral self pull in opposite directions to such an extent that the body acts on compulsion, not on the dictates of the intellect. The wishes are not being renounced but suppressed; as we shall see later, all compulsion and suppression, that is, doing a thing against our wish, is bondage, and is most unsatisfactory The point to realize at present, is that *the one and only moral wrong according to the laws of nature, is the failure of the moral self to dominate the unwise wish.*

VII

DISCRIMINATION AND BALANCE

NO human being succeeds in holding an exactly true course through life. There are, on the one hand, the short-comings of omission—the negative faults of lethargy, inertia, and laziness; on the other hand, the positive mistakes of intemperance, over-indulgence, and dissipation. Between the two there lies a balance, a realm which is neither too little nor too much, but just the amount which makes for greatest efficiency, progress, happiness, and satisfaction. The mental faculty which enables us to find the balance, is discrimination. The qualities which enable us to maintain a balance are volition and self-control.

A general knowledge of what, in a gross way, constitutes inertia and over-indulgence, is acquired early in life. Even a well trained dog is capable of some discrimination. So universal up to a certain point, is understanding in this matter that it is taken for granted that if people break the laws of society, the punishment they incur is deserved. Moreover, some experiences are so fraught with pain that they are never forgotten. These are the dramatic consequences of gross folly, where effects are so intimately associated with causes, that even a child thereby acquires sufficient discrimination never to repeat the offence.

If, however, discrimination is to be applied only to those things which lie outside the laws of man, or are forced dramatically on our attention, we may expect an unhappy existence. Quite within the law, and within the sanction and even approval of society, there are commonplace habitual shortcomings and excesses which, if we judge by the personal suffering that follows in their train, are more repugnant to nature than some offences which man punishes with penal servitude. Although all things in the world work together to promote evolution, they nevertheless hold *for man* potentialities of evil as well as good. Up to a certain point increasingly they will afford benefit; beyond that point increasingly they do harm.

Consider the food we eat. With too little nourishment, the body becomes weakly, and unable to carry out good work. With too much food, there results a poisoned state of the blood which in time may cause organic disease. Thus, positive harm will be caused by too much or too little. A considerable quantity of food might, in the case of a labourer, be just the correct amount. With another individual the same quantity might prove excess which would bring suffering. What on one occasion might be of advantage to an individual, on another might prove of disadvantage, or what at the regular time might be proper, at the wrong time might prove harmful.

The possibilities of error with regard to eating seem very alarming, but only to such as are not content to avoid extremes. There is in nature a leniency which permits the vast majority of people to derive from life a fair degree of satisfaction and happiness. It is obvious, however, that nature intends that the moral self shall develop with the intellect—that knowledge of truth shall be applied in muscular action or conduct. If we associate with those who expect us to partake of macaroons, ice cream, and chocolate at five in the afternoon, a six course dinner at seven in the evening, and a hearty supper in the early hours of the morning, without the exercise of considerable discrimination and self-control, suffering will sooner or later be inevitable.

As respects body development, the need for discrimination, volition, and control is great. Inertia soon causes the muscles to be so infiltrated with fat that fatigue follows even trivial activity. The toxins of food, improperly combusted through lack of exercise, float in the blood, cloud the intellect, and threaten the tissues. On the other hand, the muscles may be exercised so violently that they break a bone, or incapacitate the body's organs through overstrain. With a balanced amount of work, the muscles not only will afford the greatest enduring total of good, but they will develop capacity for a higher level of achievement. Only through careful individual discrimination can one find the balance, which is more or less of a sliding scale. The unbalanced going to extremes one week, with the inevitable inertia which follows in the next, not only handicaps accomplishment, but fosters discouragement and discontent.

Coming to the mental and spiritual sphere, we find the same need for discrimination if we are to have balanced minds. General mental development follows closely the laws of muscular development, but much more slowly. If the mind be inert, the associations, which we have built up in study and experience, gradually fade away and are lost. The perceptual paths in the brain which represent memory become dissociated, so that impulses no longer get through where once they travelled. The paths which have been worn the most deeply are the last to fade, and the first to go are those which represent the highest phase of development.

The parts of the mind which are of highest development, and the most recently developed parts of the brain, are the most unstable. These are the parts which first disintegrate and degenerate when causes of disintegration come into play. The moral self, which is our highest heritage, will no more than anything else remain inert. Unless we make use of the knowledge we have, the moral self disintegrates. Unless the moral self exercises its function of concentrating and driving impulses through resistant synapses or nerve centres, it remains or becomes a puerile affair, soft and flabby.

On the other hand, while general mental exertion and application with balanced control never bring harmful results, the disasters resulting from over-development in one line, with infantile conditions in another, are all too prevalent. The greater the volition, the greater must be the control. It is not sufficient to be able to accomplish; balanced development entails the ability to let go. This is where the highest powers of discrimination have their play. This is the greatest problem of life—to estimate just how much effort should be bestowed on each activity, so that we may neither overdo nor funk.

Without emotion, the body would be like a vegetable, alive, growing, and able to react to some forces like heat, and light, but incapable of recognizing or of entertaining feeling toward anything in the environment. Emotional impulses, if not too strong, lend strength and zest to all our desires. They facilitate the activity of thought, and give delight to our undertakings. Beyond the limit of control, emotional impulses incapacitate, through interfering with reason and body functions, and through rendering muscular activity inco-ordinate or even convulsive.

Without fear, we continually should be giving unbridled license to our selfish wishes, and injuring our bodies through recklessness. With uncontrolled fear, apprehensions check our progress, and even the discomfort of exertion causes us to funk. Excessive fear interferes with the functioning of the body's organs, and is capable of paralyzing movement. Balanced fear conserves our bodies, and gives us a wholesome dislike for selfishness in all its forms.

Without the instinct of combativeness and its emotion, anger, the forces of selfishness would ride roughshod over us, and we should be incapable of effectually employing our volition in the interest of justice. With too much anger we are blinded to wisdom, and act with a folly which later causes shame, regret and suffering. With balanced anger* we intelligently employ our energies to resist what is unwise, and valiantly assail the forces inimicable to our best interests.

Balanced anger is an important part of volition: balanced fear is an equally important part of control. It is quite obvious that anger and fear should be the most powerful allies of truth, but like all strong forces, they must be controlled with wise discrimination, as there are no limits to the harm they can do. When the moral self employs anger and fear with reason, they are virtues of inestimable value. Left uncontrolled by reason, they might

* It is to be recalled that, like other emotions, anger, when attenuated, forms a part of normal activity, and does not imply the excessive degree of emotion the word generally suggests.

perhaps be serviceable in jungle warfare, but they present a sorry spectacle in the sphere of spiritual accomplishment.

Excess in the activity of the reproductive instinct requires but little by way of comment. The misery, shame, and bodily suffering which come to light daily from lack of discrimination and self-control in this regard may afford an explanation for, though it does not excuse, the harmful prudishness and unhealthy mysteriousness concerning this God-given function. The desires of the awakening reproductive instinct are not devices of the devil, nor are they impulses for which we should feel shame and mortification. The unfortunate teaching which has made men and women scourge and crucify themselves, because the sexual desire awakens to consciousness, is one cause of functional nervousness in its most serious form.

It should always be made clear to early youth that sexual excitations are the natural inheritance of every healthy boy and girl; that they are to be expected as a consequence of virility, and are conditions to which youth must adapt itself, in the same way as it adapts itself to other animal impulses, namely, through self-control.

The common failing of moral teaching in this regard is to lay special stress on suppression, and largely to neglect the general function of self-control. The average mother, for example, would be horrified should her son fall to temptations of sexual appetite, but she is comparatively complacent to over-indulgence in other directions, forgetting that the ability for self-control is dependent largely on the general habit, and that the impulses of sex impose a strain on a boy's moral stamina which taxes *all* his resources in self-control.

None of us can avoid unwise desires, and our safety depends on developing the general ability to gather up the energy which would go into what is unwise, and to use it for that which is of advantage. This is employing volition in the right way to assist self-control. If by the time the stronger demands on our self-control come into play, we have not developed the habit of side-stepping the lesser temptations, there is very good reason to suppose that the stronger impulse will overpower the moral self.

Let us understand clearly that, by itself, there is no crime in the unwise impulse, especially the sensual thought and impulse. The crime consists in the indifference of a moral self which would allow the thought to remain and gather force. The time-honoured excuse that one cannot be expected to control one's thoughts holds good no longer. Nobody can think of two opposite things at one and the same time, for the energy of the brain is drained from all other perceptual systems to the one which is the point of concentration. Obviously, if the moral self enforces attention in the direction it dictates, the mind as well as the body can be disciplined.

The emotions of subjection and elation, or of negative and positive self-feeling, are balancers of each other. Too much negative self-feeling would undermine progress, through feelings of incapacity, self-depreciation, over-sensitiveness, shyness, servility, and inferiority; unlimited positive self-feeling would occasion the pride and arrogance which inevitably ride to a fall. The balance between the two affords the true basis for self-regard. This is an acute perception of imperfections and inadequacies of self, coupled with a consciousness of striving which has brought the body and mind into a closer relation with truth.

In another chapter we shall consider the tender emotion. In the same way, we might discuss the instincts of curiosity and repulsion, with their respective emotions wonder and disgust. Enough has been said, however, to make it clear that not only the emotions, but all mental processes in life, follow the same rule as material things, in that they have potentialities of good and evil, not only as respects the way in which they are employed, *but in proportion to the degree.*

No mental condition, by itself alone, can be virtuous. It is the relationship—the how, and how far it is employed in relation to other things that constitutes its value. So-called innocence, reverence, philanthropy, ambition, worship, abstinence, piety, penitence, and so on, are every day perverted to some base end. Moreover, when employed beyond the balanced degree, they become disintegrating in their unwisdom, interfere with progress, and occasion suffering. Only in so far as they are employed wisely are they virtuous. *They are benefits only to the extent that they build up.*

Neither do forces which disintegrate take account of good intention. The teaching that all is well so long as our intentions are good is indeed unfortunate. Such a belief will surely contribute to indifference to results and will place a handicap on striving after truth. It goes without saying that our intentions must be good, but this, while a first essential, is the smaller part of our responsibility in life. Our responsibility, our trust, the thing upon which our happiness, and our very existence depend, is using our discrimination, not for selfish ends whether of soul or body, but to balance our activities for the greatest service to the universal whole.

Just as discomfort results from over intensity of pleasant sensation, so virtuous conduct ceases to be virtue and becomes vice when it passes beyond the limit of rationality. Hard and fast rules of what comprise right and wrong are useless. The test of every spiritual process is found in the true answer to the question—is it integrating, or is it disintegrating? Careful discrimination alone can bring the true answer.

VIII

WISDOM AND OBJECTIVE

IF a man be devoid of wisdom, how is he to recognize truth and to follow it? At birth, we all lacked wisdom—we were without even the first rudiments of knowledge. We have observed in the brief sketch of mind development which precedes, how the young child acquires knowledge. We have seen how in the brain there develop perceptual systems which are the material sources of memory, belief, and sentiment. As sentiment and reason develop, and a value is placed on conduct, there arrives the forerunner of wisdom, "the still small voice of conscience," the sentiment for truth born of experience and knowledge. Who has not repeatedly met this harbinger of moral judgment? If a man be without wisdom, it is only because his selfish desires have caused him to ignore this stirring of truth in his being. If wisdom sufficient to peace of mind be lacking, it is only because the moral self has not made the body conform to the little knowledge of truth in the brain.

Wisdom does not come out of space, is not a benediction of the ether. It is the product of research and application. The intellect is the learned law maker who generally realizes what is right as opposed to wrong, and, when supported by the moral self, is the ruler who supports the intellect and proves through action what is wise. Increase in wisdom can come only through increase in knowledge of truth and more perfect application of that knowledge. Vision comes only through increase of wisdom. If we be blind, we can learn to see only by applying the knowledge we have.

The sum of knowledge in the world, although insignificant compared to all truth, is so huge that to confront it in its entirety would be utterly confusing and discouraging. It would be as though the iris were removed from the eye, and the whole outside world fell in a jumbled mass on the retina at one time. In seeing it all we should perceive nothing. As the iris of the eye limits the vision to a point which permits perception, so an objective in life limits the vast horizon of knowledge to a single focus which is sharply outlined, and presents a working possibility. The best any of us can do is to obtain a general idea of principles to be followed, and then to choose some definite objective and develop our knowledge in special work, more or less exclusive of the many other interesting pursuits which daily threaten to distract us.

It is fortunate that the great majority of people are compelled through necessity to exert their moral selves and to make a definite choice of a course to be followed and held to in life. Such persons have the inestimable advantage that each day's experience affords a help to the next day's striving. They become wise in their work. They not only travel somewhere, but they steer a more or less definite course. As a result, they make a success of their share in progress and incur a reward both of material pleasure and spiritual happiness.

Unfortunately the execrated goad of necessity is not realized in some cases as in others. There is a minority of people who have yet to find the necessity for an objective in life, or to hold to a chosen course. They are simply drifting. Their course is determined not by their intellects, but by the vacillating stimuli of their environments. They have, to be sure, many activities of a kind, but they fail to hold one course long enough to secure success and satisfaction.

It is not sufficient to say that a person should have a moral self sufficiently strong to initiate some course of productive activity, and to hold to it. The trouble is that a part of society, in its ideals, has utterly lost sight of the source of happiness and satisfaction, or has made the serious mistake of supposing that such is to be found in indolent pleasure. Thus it comes about that a certain prestige is often accorded to persons who consider themselves too fine to do honest work.

No matter how many the pleasures, no matter what the luxury, if unhappiness is to be avoided, not only must there be an objective in life, but through that objective in one way or another duty to the universe must be daily met. Just as the lower animal by disregarding the prompting of its instincts sacrifices its life, so human beings suffer when they disobey the demands of existence. To accept relief from duty in order to favour indolence or to promote unproductive hobbies will not only deprive one of happiness and satisfaction, but sooner or later may lead to definite suffering. The demand of evolution is inviolate—produce and be happy; dissipate and suffer.

Women are handicapped by having a more dependent position in life. The mistaken kindness of affording freedom from regular duties which require effort, has made it difficult for some women to escape an over-protection which is as belittling to their moral selves as it is injurious to their bodies. One reaction to this false ideal of freedom from domestic duty is to be seen in the increasing unpopularity of the sphere which, above all others, nature has intended for woman—the sphere of motherhood and service in the home.

If a young woman have freedom to choose an objective in life, she will do well to consider carefully whether her choice is such as will enable her to pursue her occupation in harmony with nature—whether she will, in fact, by actual study and personal experience, make herself efficient for the high calling of motherhood, and service to husband and children in the home. It should be a matter of grave concern that the tendency of to-day is so largely for women to choose the factory, the shop, the office, the club, the social whirl, politics, or anything that claims their interest, apart from their natural calling.

Perhaps it is sufficient to say that *men* must be brought to realize not only that the woman who habitually idles away her time is defying the demand of nature, and will bring suffering on others as well as on herself, but that the woman who scientifically carries out her duty to the home, with all that the word implies, is worthy of greater reverence and respect than he who in virtue of his home training, becomes a great ruler.

Results of real worth are never achieved haphazardly. To arrive anywhere, to achieve anything of value, there must be an objective which is maintained, not for a day or a week, but for years at a time. Self-respect is in great measure dependent upon consciousness of accomplishment, and try as we will, we cannot, year in and year out, continue to fool ourselves. Social standing may engender pride and a pretension of self-respect, but these, apart from true worth, produce far more suffering than satisfaction.

Once we have a proper objective, and strive to reach it, life takes on a new meaning. Confusion and discouragement prove but transitory. Things in general become secondary; they contribute to the one aim. Objects, events, and people become so ordered as to further the chief objective, and system thus becomes established. Each mistake becomes valuable as an aid to the next day's fuller accomplishment. In a short time the fruits of striving make their appearance, and the reward of well-spent days manifests itself in an abiding inner sense of worthiness and satisfaction.

From nature's standpoint it is better that a man follow a mistaken course than none at all. In the mistaken course, he who is half awake is sure to become wise from experience, and to develop stamina in the undertaking, whereas, without action, a man sooner or later loses the stuff which constitutes volition. One may be a paragon of negative holiness, the type of person who is abstemious, pure, and without sin, but unless he be doing something that counts, the hollowness of his holiness is as unproductive to himself as it is to the world.

If we are to grow wise through experience, whether it be in work or in play, we must use our discrimination and act on it. Discrimination is not a matter of faith or a blessing which comes merely for the asking. It is a matter of exertion of the intellect in analysis of experience, particularly our unpleasant experiences.

There are two ways in which to meet an unpleasant experience—a subjective way or an objective way—the way of feeling, or the way of reason. In the former, the experience is regarded as an affront; all the animal desires to bite and scratch and hurt in retaliation, are stimulated throughout the body; fear, or the necessity for decency, alone prevents an encounter, and a depressive emotional tone overwhelms the body, until the unpleasant feeling of the experience is effaced by other impulses from the outside world. When memory of the experience recurs, in lesser degree the depression returns, and naught but an inhibiting effect is gained through this envoy of wisdom.

On the other hand, the way of reason is to regard the unpleasant experience as something which indicates a departure from truth, somewhere—an experience to which on the next occasion, we must adapt ourselves. Of course the great probability is that the departure from truth is on the part of the other fellow! Many of us in two minutes can discover in another a fault which, in ourselves, has lain hidden for a lifetime. In the matter of faults and mistakes, the temptation is strong to interest ourselves more on another's behalf than on our own. Here is one instance where we best further general progress by giving our whole thought to ourselves, and by allowing the other person to take care of himself, at least until such time as we have carefully examined our *own* needs.

The question always should be—"What is *my* mistake in this matter; what actually is the truth; what have *I* misapplied; where have *I* fallen short or gone to excess?" If only we would spend in this direction one-half the energy we employ in endeavouring to compel recognition of righteousness in ourselves, we should develop sufficient wisdom to supply our general needs in life.

If we would retain our bodily health, and develop mental stamina, each for himself must shoulder the responsibility of general discrimination between what, for him, in every thought and every deed, is too much, and what too little, and develop the stuff to act on his discrimination. If we were to institute a regular time in the day to examine its various experiences, or if we would but occupy our spare moments reflecting on our own mistakes, not the mistakes of others, and set our course for the future by the lessons they bring, we should convert the invidious bumps of life into its greatest blessings. It is in this way that the moral self prevents the same mistake occurring over and over; in this way the mind gains its balance.

The power to discriminate requires both volition and control—volition to seek truth, and control of feeling which renders the search possible. Nothing so blinds a man to truth as excessive emotion. Nothing so stifles the right sort of introspection as unbalanced positive self-feelings, or excessive self-righteousness. We have seen that volition and control are functions of the moral self, and just in proportion as we exert ourselves in these two directions do we achieve a balance comprising rationality and power.

When, along with virile volition to serve and

co-operate, we develop rigid control, which is the ability to give up what is unwise, the brain steadily gains new powers of perception and moral judgment, and with them a strong sentiment of self-regard. Our happiness in life very largely depends on our regard for ourselves—that is to say on the extent to which we measure up to true ideals, and to which we save ourselves the great strain of pretending to be something we are not.

Nothing is more prevalent than that appearance of self-regard which obviously is based on untrue idealism, and is known as egotism or false pride. In such cases, possibly away from the clear cut light of perception, there is the dejected realization that truth is lacking, and that without worldly advantage, life would be sadly barren. No matter how successful one may be in bluffing the world, or how hard one may try to persuade himself that untruth is truth, the sentiment of self-regard depends on the consciousness of worth within. Happiness or satisfaction is one thing which must be earned. It cannot be the gift of a rich relative.

No matter what else enters into our philosophy, the aim of every living soul should be to develop, on the one hand, a virile volition which wholeheartedly strives towards the fullest accomplishment; on the other, to establish an automatic control which drops dispassionately all that is excessive, all that is tainted, all that is unwise. There may be rewards for wisdom in another world beyond our ken, but this we know for a fact that, here and now, the effort of volition and control pays in a maximum of bodily health, sensuous pleasure, and spiritual happiness. All that has been written of the hell of selfishness, and the glorious heaven of wisdom, is a living reality in this world to-day.

PART II

FACTS IGNORED

IX

IMPULSE AND REACTION

HAVING read through seven rather intricate chapters, in an effort to gain some little understanding of the workings of the mind, you are now in a position the better to appreciate how it is that anything so illusive as the moral self can be responsible for bodily fatigue or actual pain. While it is not intended to spend much time over symptoms, it is well to understand clearly whence they come. Had you known this in the beginning, possibly you would have so directed your course as never to have suffered from "nerves." And yet it is improbable that any one ever goes through life without, at times, experiencing sensations recognized as unwarranted by the particular circumstances which occasion them—feelings commonly known as nervousness.

Except in so far as mental symptoms are the outcome of some organic injury to the body, they all emanate from the one cause. While the manifestations of nervousness are as changeable as the views of a kaleidoscope, they all have a starting place at one focus. The severity of symptoms is but an indication of the degree to which the cause is operative, and the permanent relief of any and every symptom is dependent, not on medicine, but on a clear understanding of the cause, and an earnest wrestling with it.

The cause, as already stated, is found in a moral self which inadequately fulfils its function of volition and control. It is not, however, so much in single actions by themselves that nervousness finds its origin, as in certain oft-repeated reactions to things, conditions, people, and thoughts —reactions which usually continue to operate from childhood, and sooner or later misadapt one to his environment.

As in the lives of the lower animals, the greater part of our lives, try as we will, is spent in reaction to the things and conditions about us. The energy of our bodies travels so much more easily along the inborn nerve paths that it is only through habitual effort on the part of the moral self that we are able, as we grow older, to discipline impulses, and to be comparatively independent of the suggestions of the environment.

We have seen that the animal is compelled to obey the impulse; in other words, to act on the feeling which each thing or condition in its environment affords. If man were deprived of his moral self, he would act on the same basis of compulsion as the animal, and it may readily be understood that the less the moral self asserts itself, the nearer one approaches the compulsion basis.

Of course, there are times in the lives of each of us, when the indication is, as we say, to take a holiday—when it is wise to relax, and, within certain limits, to allow the mind lazily to follow its inclinations. Possibly this may be indicated for a portion of each day to balance mental concentration during the working hours. When, however, through lack of necessity, or through disinclination to exert itself, the moral self is given more or less of a continuous holiday, it loses power.

Consider an instance, familiar to most of us, of the way the habit of reacting to the impulse or the feelings suggested by things in the environment asserts itself where the moral self is but feebly exercised. Breakfast is over, and the good housewife proceeds to the clearing of the table, when a loud noise occurs on the street. The feeling of curiosity gains ascendancy, and a visit to the front window is indulged in. The front window happens to present a particularly dirty smudge which commands extinction, and, forthwith, it is removed. Just as this is accomplished, Mrs. Vanity Fair is seen issuing from her front door a few houses away, and the impulse to ask her about the committee meeting of The Woman's Efficiency League becomes overwhelming. While the housewife is talking with Mrs. Vanity Fair, the postman happens along with a letter from Jim's brother's wife;

it insists on being read without delay. And so it goes, perhaps a little more so, perhaps a little less.

There is nothing very terrible in all this, and quite possibly you feel that the little housewife was not compelled at all by the noise in the street, the smudge on the window, Mrs. Vanity Fair's appearance, and the letter from Jim's brother's wife. If not compelled, why does she act on the stimulus? You answer, simply because she wishes to. Admitting this to be so, the matter of compulsion is only switched from the thing which stimulated the wish to the wish itself; in either case it was the impulse started by the suggestion which compelled the action. You protest that the housewife did not *have* to obey the impulse, that she could have overcome it. Such, fortunately, is the case, because her moral self still has the power to assert itself, and, while the habit of constant reaction threatens to swamp the moral self, the stage has not been reached in which the actual *have to* prevails.

You are not satisfied. You cannot see why, if the little housewife wishes to do these things, she has not a perfect right to. Her circumstances did not make it necessary for her to tire herself; she was not hurting anybody, and quite possibly her good husband had said: "By all means, my dear, take it easy, and enjoy yourself." Let it be repeated, our object is not to find fault; it is to point the way to health and happiness. Many habits which man condones and even encourages, nature punishes severely. This habit of taking the line of least resistance is one of them. Women as well as men have a responsibility to nature, if not to people. Any one who habitually fritters away his time in gratification of selfish wishes, to the neglect of the development of volition and self-control, sacrifices happiness and self-respect.

The housewife has not reached the length of incapacity to control her unwise wishes, and undoubtedly her easy yielding to them is purely the result of her habit of acting on impulsive feeling instead of on principle. Dr. McDougall points out, however, that "*the first step toward moral conduct is the control of the immediate impulse,*" and in allowing the impulse to dictate to her she is travelling towards bondage, toward the place where her moral self will become so impoverished from inactivity that the things of life will gain an extraordinary power over her.

It is the insidiousness, the apparent right of the thing, that constitutes its danger. No one would think of criticising a little housewife for anything so innocent, and where in the name of Heaven is she to receive instruction on this most vital of life's concerns? Her husband tells her it is what he wishes; the Church for the greater part lays more stress on faith and belief than on commonplace living and doing, and those who realize the truth, diplomatically or discreetly mind their own business. Let all who are disposed to find fault with the helplessness of nervousness after the damage is done, question as to their own indifference to causes which promote it.

It is not intended to convey the idea that the sort of habitual reaction described is a symptom of nervousness. To the extent exemplified in the housewife, it is only a cause, but a very prevalent cause. It requires no stretch of the imagination to realize that this habit may lead to actual compulsions, where patients state that they feel forced to follow some unreasonable behaviour, such as wearing a water-proof cloak in bed, or collecting pictures, silks, perchance precious stones, while lacking the means for ordinary living purposes. It will be recognized that the unreasonable purchase of luxuries to gratify whims, belongs to the same category.

Another habitual reaction of a compulsory nature, familiar to most of us, is found in the inability to put aside a thing, or to cease an activity, when it is reasonable so to do. An appointment might have been at hand, or the family might have been holding the customary indignation meeting at the dinner table, but day after day one thing or another, which quite readily could have been attended to later, "just *had* to be finished." Something which stimulates a feeling wins out over what, if the moral self were employed, would be acted upon as reasonable and wise. In the chronically late person, the habit again betrays itself, for in such an individual you will always find a moral self which is abnormally subservient to things in the environment. The inability to throw away or destroy all sorts of worthless junk is another indication of a self which lacks rational decision and action.

Allow this subservience of the moral self to become extreme, and you meet with a state of affairs which is obviously pathological, as in an individual who hesitates for hours before being able to cross a street, about which he entertains some foolish feeling, or again, as in one who feels unable to decide independently whether to wear a pink or a blue undershirt.

If inanimate objects in the environment can gain an impelling influence over conduct, what will become of the weakened self in coping with commanding personalities? Existence is liable to take on a character more or less goaded. For the greater part the activities of life come to be followed because circumstances, or some one other than oneself, wills or commands, not because one's spirit or wish is in the matter.

How often we say, "I never have a moment to do a thing I wish!" Accepting the statement at its doubtful face value, why is this so? Simply because we do not wish to do the things we should. They are being done in opposition to the wish, in other words, on a compulsion basis. If the things we are doing are not wise and right, we are at fault, irrespective of who commands that they be done. On the other hand, if it be wise and rational to carry out a given work—if, in view of what is our rightful part in cooperation, we consider it to be fair, and regard the work as our duty—is it not selfishness to wish to do otherwise?

Right here is the crux of the whole matter of nervousness. Are our wishes to be in accord with what is reasonable, or are we to be *forced* to do what is reasonable, and kick against the pricks every step of the way? If wholeheartedly we enter into the spirit of what it is reasonable and wise to do, if, in other words, we ally our wishes with what is true, we shall gain personal power and happiness. If, on the other hand, we struggle continually against what is reasonable and wise, if our wishes are constantly at war with what has to be, we shall become embittered and worn out by depressive emotions. What has to be, is a fixture to which our mobile wishes are to be adapted by the moral self.

You feel that this would be all very well could you deal with your wishes as one would with a machine, but the fact is that when you really wish a thing, you feel you cannot help wishing it. Let us be very frank on this point, because it is the vital one in self-control. If you cannot give up a wish when it is wise that you should do so, you have not practised self-control as freely as you should.

In ability to renounce we all have our limitations; viewed from a slightly different angle, it has been said: "Every man has his price." Sometimes it is money, sometimes social prestige, and sometimes it is gratification of feelings of inertia or of animal appetite. *The facility with which we can forego our unwise wishes is proportional to the amount of our practice in this regard.*

If you call the roll on your various wishes, there are many of them which, you freely confess, you could give up with very little difficulty. There are others about which you have your doubts, and still others which, wise or unwise, no matter if the bottom fell out of Heaven, you would not let go. There is no royal road to moral stamina; it comes only through making a habit of wise volition and renunciation.

You ask—" Suppose I regard the work I have to do as excessive, and, for that reason, wish for more recreation?" If the work actually be excessive, the excessive part is unwise. In this enlightened twentieth century there is no bondage other than the thralldom of the moral self. What are the circumstances; who is there who would dominate your moral self, and make it submit to what is unwise? A characteristic of excessive positive self-feeling is the over-importance we attach to the part we play in life. Every day it is demonstrated that the world, the community, the family, or the individual, *can* negotiate without our services. To be sure it is sometimes very inconvenient, but our sentiment for truth, our determination to do what is wise at all costs, should disregard inconvenience, displeasure, or anything else.

The fact of the matter is that, in the great majority of instances, what is fair and right, when reasonably presented, carries of itself the power to prevail. Usually it is opposing wishes which make work seem excessive, or, if it actually be excessive, it is a mistaken self-interest or a false pride which keeps it so. How often, believing herself to be unselfish, a woman ruins her health, because she feels compelled to do what she realizes is unwise. The world may admire, but there is no question as to how nature regards such conduct. Results speak for themselves. Because the moral code of society in many places has either lost sight of the requirements of nature, or does not permit a sufficiently free expression of such requirements, much unnecessary suffering has come upon civilized peoples.

How many a man, impelled by a selfish wish for money, prestige, or fame, has not the time to do what is wise. He contends, of course, that his unwisdom is for the advantage of others, and in some way that is supposed to make irrationality right. How comforting at times is sophistry! Is it not the fact that the man's wish or ambition is to him a thing bigger than either wisdom or truth? The part to be noted particularly is that when he is tired, over-wrought, or ill, as a consequence of his irrationality, he is disposed to regard this as something to his credit rather than as deliberate intemperance.

So habituated have we become to untrue ways of

thinking, that simply to point out these things to the man who allows his wishes to override reason, will occasion prejudice and even irritability. In the matter of work, nature, before interfering, grants a wide margin to the healthy body. Overwork in itself is responsible for considerably less suffering than is inertia. That in this direction, however, lack of self-control *is* an offense against nature, let the consequences again speak for themselves.

While the vast majority of men and women will freely admit, and even aver, that wise conduct is of advantage, consciously or sub-consciously each entertains a reservation in his own particular case, as to when the theory is to be applied. Each has exceptional experiences where he feels it would not pay to be wise, and the fact is, so far as mere material gain is concerned, it often does not pay.

Until people have tasted of spiritual triumph, until they have come to realize that there is a happiness of soul with which material pleasures cannot compare—a condition of mind which acts as an anti-toxin to suffering—how can their point of view be otherwise? The threat of a hell or the promise of reward in a heaven on the other side of the grave, is too remote in its appeal. Men know all about hell here on earth. What they need is education and persuasion about a heaven, equally attainable, here and now. If they realize *that,* the other heaven may be left to take care of itself.

X

UNHEALTHY MENTAL HABITS

THE less the moral self makes a habit of employing volition in looking for the truth in people's statements, the more are they accepted at their face value and the more do they cause reaction to the untruth as well as the truth which they contain. Reason tells us that the only thing about which we need be concerned is truth, but the mind with the undeveloped moral self places far more faith in impression. To the person whose intellect is not employed in discrimination, it matters little about the truth of what is said, as long as the *feeling* produced is pleasant. By the strong mind, on the other hand, even flattery will be resented as a reflection on one's habits of thought.

When, in a marked degree, the moral self fails to check the childish habit of reacting to the feeling rather than to the truth of what is said, it is not long before symptoms of nervousness begin to show themselves, especially among those who move in a complex social sphere. Such persons, although psychically undeveloped, are nevertheless treated as adults. When subjected to snobbishness, sarcasm, and other diabolical methods of mental torture, seemingly delighted in by some members of society, their emotions only, and not their intellect, come into play. What is even worse, without making the effort to derive the true meaning out of what is said, or even the intended meaning, such persons jump to the conclusions which their particular brand of feeling causes them to *suppose* is meant.

Is there need to speak of sensitiveness, of painful self-consciousness, depressive moods, and feelings of inadequacy and inferiority, when these conditions prevail? Is it necessary to point out that under such conditions the emotional tone is no longer in the keeping of the moral self, but is the plaything of every comer? We find, as a result, all kinds of abnormal *defense reactions*. One individual, for example, will become so silent that nobody can get an opportunity to criticise his opinions. Another will talk so continuously that it is obvious she sub-consciously is apprehensive, and seeks to save the situation.

If an excessive negative self-feeling is a result of the moral self failing to exert itself in a search for truth in statements of others, much more so is an exaggerated positive self-feeling an outcome of the same thing. The very fact that sub-consciously, if not consciously, we realize that our moral self is weak and requires protection, makes us ready to resist with vigor or to put up a defense against all supposed or real attacks. The instincts of self-preservation, namely, combativeness and flight, are quick to come to the rescue. To resist attack successfully we must make ourselves feel that we are in the right. Consequently, over and over again, we assure ourselves that we *are* right, we proclaim our righteousness to those around us, or we run away, and refuse to discuss the issue.

Gradually there is built up an iron-clad positive self-feeling which assails, but is unassailable. In this way there comes the unbalanced state of mind where, in some directions, there are overwrought negative self-feelings, with dejection, discouragement, and despondency, and in other directions, there are positive self-feelings so exalted that need for reformation would not be admitted for a moment.

When this state of affairs is reached, the habitual reactions to fair and unfair criticisms, to taunts, and conversational jibes of all kinds, is familiar to everybody. Of course it varies in degree, and we all have our limit, but when a degree is reached where a well educated individual can be thrown into a paroxysm of emotional distress by the jibe of an ignorant underling, it is time to take stock of just what part the moral self is playing in the matter of adaptation. It is human to have outbursts of temper when circumstances become exasperating, but it is also human to profit by experience, and when the same violent reaction over and over again follows the same circumstances, it is becoming something other than wholesome indignation.

Such habitual reactions may go to the length that they become pathological disabilities in themselves, or, as we shall see presently, they may occasion illness through interfering with the functions of the body's organs.

It is not only the contact with people that stimulates such unfortunate reactions. Even when away from others, undirected impulses wandering at random through the archives of the brain, continue to harass the impoverished self. When volition is not employed in directing the energy of the mind, persistent thoughts, unhappy memories and foolish apprehensions make of the body a tragedian puppet which stages a phantasy of gloom. So it is that " Life is a tragedy to those who feel, and a comedy to those who think."

The habit of accepting without analysis one's own fancies and thoughts operates in the same manner as with statements of others. The thought, like the statement, is received on feeling rather than on reason. To apply truth to thought requires much effort when it is not a habit. Consequently thoughts which are unpleasant or painful become suppressed; they are not analyzed so as to get at their truth or untruth. We shall presently consider the baneful effect on the mind of suppression of thoughts.

The moral self which finds great difficulty in controlling reactions of the body to impulses occasioned by objects and people, usually finds it impossible to overcome at least the feeling produced by thoughts. The meaning of the thought may not be perceived consciously, but the feeling is there, and works its unhappy influence. So it is that thoughts, pleasant or unpleasant, reasonable or unreasonable, become insubordinate to the moral self, demand recognition, and impel action on the part of the body.

Familiar to everybody is the type of mother (and we all love her) whose maternal instinct produces feelings which quite outweigh reason. She will admit that she knows it is foolish to worry about her boy, who is delayed from getting home from work, but she simply cannot dismiss the unreasonable apprehensions which dominate her mind.

Let it be made clear: Fears which are based on reason are normal, and useful in their protective potentialities. Nervous apprehension exists only when fears are unreasonable, or are in excess of what is rational.

It is unnecessary to use time or space to enlarge upon unreasonable thoughts and feelings such as, at times, assail the minds of all of us. All worry consists of thoughts of this type. When unreasonable thoughts come, as inevitably they will, it is fortunate if they can be met by a virile moral self—a self sufficiently commanding to set the mind to work at something useful, instead of allowing it to stew in the fires of its irrational feelings.

When the moral self is undeveloped or reaches a

degree of excessive incapacity in dealing with thoughts, it is a matter of little wonder that persons acquire ideas which, to their satisfaction, cannot be proved unreasonable. It is not surprising, in other words, that thoughts become organized into more or less fixed beliefs, and constitute scruples and obsessions. Because of some breach of social etiquette, for example, one man comes to feel so strongly that everybody is disposed to ostracise him that no amount of reasoning can dissuade him. Every day he finds evidence which he *feels* supports his belief, and so it grows. Some woman who has been accidentally omitted from an entertainment becomes convinced, in spite of all evidence to the contrary, that the hostess is her mortal enemy. Another implicitly believes that his stomach is diseased, and, in spite of expert advice, continues to make himself sick with medicine and through introspection of his body feelings. We all at times have irrational feelings, and we should be ready to sympathize with any one whose moral self is too weak to come to his rescue.

Not only do irrational thoughts in themselves become symptoms of "nerves," but, in several ways, they may produce bodily disability. While emotions produced by irrational thoughts do not necessarily cause violent outbursts, such as are characteristic of some habitual reactions we have considered, they may be of a more constantly depressing nature, and, as such, are just as instrumental as are emotional fireworks in causing bodily disability.

The reactions we have considered—including impulsiveness, hyper-sensitiveness, self-consciousness, shyness, impatient irritability, fretfulness, violent outbursts of temper, depressive moods, apprehension, illogical doubts and scruples, worry, irrational fears of all kinds, introspection of body feelings and functions—when persistently indulged in, become unhealthy mental habits. No matter what the intellect may be, all of these habits in themselves, comprise symptoms of nervousness, and, in some individuals, may go further, and cause disturbance in the functions of the body's organs as well. All these unfortunate reactions are indulged in because an undeveloped or lazy moral self fails to exercise control, and, in some instances has permitted the organization of abnormal mental complexes.

A *complex* is a nervous energy path organization which may be activated by the stimulus of a suggestion as contained, for example, in a thought, a sight, or a condition. A complex may be simply a system of associated memories with their attendant emotions, as described in Chapter III, or, as we shall see presently, linked up with the memory system the organization may include energy paths concerned with other functions.

A complex, when normal, that is, when based on truth, is serviceable to the body, but when the reverse it is a handicap. When memory systems include distorted perceptions of things, conditions, sayings, happenings, and people, that is, when they are complexes fouled by untruth, they are the source of much unhappiness. Whenever they are stimulated by some associated thought, object or condition, the feelings which they activate come into play.

We all have abnormal complexes which survive for varying lengths of time. Some of them people describe as "sore points" which arise through "having it rubbed in." The person with the active moral self usually takes the trouble in his calm moments to examine painful complexes, and to apply common sense to the fantasy of misconception they contain, and so puts them out of business. The sluggish self, on the other hand, often lets them lie until they fade from consciousness. If their impression be deep, their unhappy effect in the sub-conscious mind will be felt when they are stimulated.

You perhaps have been told that you are too introspective, too self-absorbed. There are two kinds of introspection, a very wrong kind and a right kind. To dwell on *feelings* which arise from complexes can only produce harm, but to examine and analyze the complexes themselves, and to apply truth to them, is invaluable to peace of mind. While you cannot find the complexes formed in childhood or those which have since become subconscious, you can treat the ones of which you are conscious by using your own common sense or the philosophy of some one else. To examine complexes is not pleasant. It necessitates exposure to your own consciousness of things in yourself which are uncomplimentary. The majority of people automatically resist doing this very thing. The line of least resistance for all of us is to repose comfortably in a feeling of self-righteousness, but it does not pay.

That depressive thoughts and emotions uncontrolled by the moral self *can* cause interference with the working of the body's organs is a fact too generally recognized to require much in the way of substantiation. You have only to recall the body adjustments which, in Chapter II, you saw took place under the stress of fear, to realize how this comes about. A few instances of the effect of the depressive emotions on the body may prove convincing.

There is a medicine prepared from a certain kind of cockroach which, when dispensed with other tonic preparations, is sometimes very effective as a sedative to the stomach in cases of nervous dyspepsia. However, let an individual with sensitive disposition come across the body of a cockroach in a bowl of soup of the contents of which he has just partaken, and his digestion not only is likely to be arrested, but his stomach may react violently to the psychic condition. Obviously, if the cockroach were not thought about, its presence might serve as a sedative rather than as an emetic.

If you recall the sudden death of a dear friend, or some particularly shocking experience, you will probably remember the effect it had on your digestion. Quite possibly you felt you could not eat; by the dryness of the mouth, the salivary glands seemed to have discontinued operations, and the little food you managed to swallow, being inadequately digested, added to the sombreness of your depression.

In the silent watches of the night you may have heard the stair creak with a suggestion ominous of burglars. If, instead of using your volition and going to investigate, you kept very still, the emotion of fear gained ascendancy over the moral self, and your heart nearly choked you with the violence of its beating, your muscular energy ebbed away, leaving you abjectly weak, and the sweat glands all over your body became, of a sudden, remarkably active. Is there any doubt in your mind that in this instance a thought, with its accompanying emotion, was responsible for the disturbance of the functions of the heart, the muscles, and the sweat glands? Are you of the opinion that the body symptoms experienced under these circumstances were all imagination, that you did not actually suffer disturbance of the functions? Do you think that a sojourn at the seaside would prevent these symptoms from recurring under similar provocation? By no means. A little medicine might brace you up temporarily, but if an upset of the kind is to be avoided in the future, it is the moral self, not the body, which requires attention.

A Russian scientist, Dr. J. P. Pavlov, has carried out some very enlightening experiments on animals, to prove the effect of mind over body. Among other things, he has found by actual observation of the internal organs of living dogs that pleasurable emotions, as excited by sight of choice morsels of food, will cause secretion of digestive juices in the stomach; that joyous expectations, such as the anticipation of a romp, will activate peristalsis; and that depressive emotions, such as are occasioned by a threatened whipping, will have an opposite effect on the stomach and intestines.

Pavlov has shown also that when feeding a dog, by repeatedly associating a peculiar noise with a certain kind of food, he can bring about the same effect on the dog's internal organs either by allowing him to hear the peculiar noise or by giving him a sight of the food. In other words, through education he establishes a complex in the dog's mind, whereby the memory system comprising sight of food and peculiar noise is associated with certain nervous energy paths going to the stomach and intestines. The function or work of the complex is to stimulate all its parts when activated in any of its associations.

These facts applied to people mean that the functions of their organs are affected not only by certain sights and sounds, but by the hundred and one memories which, through education or by accident, have become associated. For example, a particularly emotional young lady happens to be a passenger in a train which is wrecked, and her emotions so burn the horrifying circumstances into her memory that an abnormal complex becomes organized. For some time after the wreck, the functions of her body are interfered with. There are sudden startings-up from sleep, a feeling of great muscular weakness, a feeling of compulsion to throw her hand up to her face, as though to ward off a blow, and possibly other effects. As time goes on the symptoms subside, and she manages to fill her mind with other activities. Without necessarily recalling the memory of the experience, because the memory often is suppressed and not willingly examined, the toot of a steam engine, the meeting with a person who looks like somebody in the wreck, the touch of a plush cushion, the smell of soft coal smoke, anything associated with the wreck, quite possibly may cause a return of the old time symptoms. The cure, of course, is found in strengthening the moral self to the place where it can adapt the mind and the body to the memory.

Aside from the context, but of great interest to everybody, and especially to our legal friends, is the question—Should a railway company be liable for damages for this kind of disability? Who is responsible? It would seem that the disability need not have occurred, had there been no railroad accident; on the other hand, if the moral self had been normally virile, it need not have occurred, notwithstanding the accident.

In addition to common experience and the experiments of Pavlov, there is the fact that, in the hypnotized subject, that is, in a person whose moral self is rendered temporarily subordinate, disturbances of function can be artificially produced and removed at the will or suggestion of the operator. For example, functional paralysis of a limb, which is a condition where the subject is unable not only to move the limb, but even to feel needles inserted into the flesh can be produced or removed with a spoken suggestion. The blood vessels can be made to dilate and cause a flush, or, through contraction, produce lividity. The stomach can be made to eject its contents, or to recover from an attack of indigestion. Abject depression and grief can be instituted, or thoughts which have been harassing the body, can be removed, and, in their place, there can be substituted ideas which are uplifting and energizing, all at the suggestion of the operator.

While in the case of the hypnotized subject, suggestion accomplishes its purpose with ease, the individual whose moral self is in extreme subservience to objects, conditions, and people in his environment, is not so far removed from the hypnotized state that suggestions, whether intentional or accidental, whether wise or foolish, fail to excite a haphazard influence over his mind and body.

Perhaps the most delightful and convincing proof of all with regard to the influence of the mind over the body, is the fact that disturbance of body function through unhealthy mental habits and abnormal complexes, clears up of its own accord when the complexes are exposed to common sense, and the habits are overcome by a strengthened moral self.

It may readily be understood that where untrue complexes are being continually built up in the mind, the environment becomes filled with people who are constantly stimulating unhappy and depressive emotions. Under such circumstances, to get away from everybody and everything, under the care of some one who can trace the reactions to the complexes from which they arise, and who is artful in applying truth to them in attractive form, will afford much relief. This, however, is dealing only with the past. An even more important task is the development of volition and control for the future. Of such a nature is the work of the psycho-therapeutist, a work which in its prophylactic possibilities is the most promising, albeit the least developed, of any branch of medical science.

XI

SUGGESTION AND SUGGESTIBILITY

TO some degree every person is open to suggestion. With the little child suggestion, sympathy, and imitation underlie its every action, and until reason has been acquired, conduct is largely the outcome of suggestion, which is the invitation or command of the environment. Children are particularly open to suggestion, because they have not had the experiences which develop reason and make them cautious. As they grow older, they find that suggestion may be of untruth as well as truth, and they tend more and more to apply reason to suggestion before acting upon it. The more they become exposed to the wiles of the world, the less they accept suggestion on its face value. The more protected they have been, the less likely they are to apply reason, because they have found less need to do so. In all of us, however, the innate tendency is there, and, to a higher or lower degree, suggestion tends always to work itself out to fulfillment.

It is not well to be a materialist, the type of person who will not accept anything he cannot perceive with his senses, because after all, science itself is founded on imagination, and the senses are very limited in perception. On the other hand, it is necessary that reason should be applied to all suggestion, and that faith should have some support on fact. The habitual gullibility which swallows truth and untruth without discrimination, some day will bring trouble to the body as well as to the mind, and it will be difficult to convince the sufferer of the cause. If there be one indication greater than all others in the furtherance of mental health, it is to apply reason to any and every suggestion, before it is accepted as capital stock in the business of living.

Suggestion may have its origin, as has been described in the preceding chapters, through objects, conditions, and people, or in one's own mind. The shop window is full of suggestions, the sunshiny day offers its suggestion of buoyancy, and the cloudy day its suggestion of gloom. Not a day passes without its quota of wise and unwise suggestions from our friends and more particularly from our relatives, and with every hour auto-suggestion, or the suggestion evolved in our own minds, gives us the impulse to do all sorts of wise and unwise acts.

While the suggestibility of a person depends on the weakness of the moral self, that is, on the complacency with which feeling is permitted to rule the self, in the same individual it varies from time to time, according to the state of mind. When the mind is tired, the effort to reason is naturally in abeyance, and suggestion is admitted with less resistance.

The wish in the mind at the time the suggestion comes into play is a most important factor. For example, the wish to avoid some activity would afford the auto-suggestion, " I am tired or ill," an excellent opportunity to take hold, did the reasoning query, " Am I really tired or ill? " not interfere. Again, in an individual with a sentiment favourable to fine clothes, liveried footmen, and pomp, such things would possess a power of putting across a suggestion which an anarchist would laugh to scorn.

The circumstances under which a suggestion is offered, that is, the setting in which it is presented, is important. For example, the soft music, the dim lights, the soothing chant of the church service, all afford a setting for the suggestion in the sermon. Every woman thoroughly understands the atmosphere in which to bring to her husband's attention the suggestion about the latest thing from Paris, and every business man knows something of the psychic factors entering into advertisements and contracts. Business interests also understand the power of repetition and persuasion, for day after day, the gullible public is being duped by things which were unconsidered or refused in the beginning, but which happen along at the time when the moral self is temporarily vulnerable.

If the moral self be vulnerable to one type of

suggestion more than another, it is to suggestion relating to the human body. No matter what his other interests in life, there is none greater to man than that of his own body. The temptation to talk about oneself and one's feelings is paramount, and this field of conversation is replete with perverted ideas about the body.

If by chance the body begins to suffer from bad mental habits, the mind more than ever is on the *qui vive* for other people's aches and pains. With attention in this direction aroused, there develops a pseudo sympathy, so congenial to the sufferer of every kind that he feels disposed to enlarge upon all the details of his ailment. Obviously, this is harmful both to speaker and listener. The former through auto-suggestion and repetition, renders more vivid, possibly magnifies, and drives home details of suffering which he should do his best to forget; to the listener, whose sympathy really is intense interest in his own body, each detail comes as a suggestion of possible trouble in his own case.

Of all compelling desires, there probably is none as universal as the wish to talk about personal troubles. As one lady put it, " I just have to get my troubles off my chest," and no amount of argument could make her believe that she was seeking gratification of a selfish wish. Possibly you, also, find it difficult to see where the selfishness comes in. Only that which builds up and is of advantage to progress is wise. No matter how intended, that which pulls down or disintegrates is unwise. Knowingly to do that which is unwise, and which therefore is not for the advantage of all, is selfish. If one will allow his reason to dominate his wish for a minute, he must see that to talk of trouble, merely to gratify a feeling, is to disregard the accentuation of suffering, and pulling-down effect, which is inevitable.

Memory is sensation, if only a fraction of the original, and to accentuate the memory of suffering is to suffer over again to a limited extent. This is demonstrated in the child who cries the second time when recording his memory of a painful happening. The one who tells of his suffering, suffers again, and according to the suggestibility of the person listening, his emotional tone, that is, his quality of feeling, approximates that of the first individual. Is there any good in all this? Certainly there is considerable harm.

You are not satisfied. You feel that somewhere there is relief gained. If you be unable to discriminate between relief and gratification of a wish, let us for argument's sake regard them as one and the same thing, for undoubtedly there is temporary relief of a kind in the gratification of any and every wish. Do you then consider that you would be justified in exacting relief from your own troubles at another's expense? You answer—" What if the other person has no objection?" If you would ascertain beforehand whether the other person has any objection to hearing your troubles, considerable gloom would undoubtedly be avoided. Suppose, however, one were foolish enough to allow you to destroy his property because you had a wish to obtain something which you could get only by doing damage, should you be justified in so doing? Look at it how you will, it resolves itself at best into the old time question: is it right to do wrong that good may come of it? In this instance, the good which may come is imaginary, not real. The only real thing about it is the harm which inevitably results.

On the other hand, analysis of trouble with the view of avoiding a similar occurrence in the future, not only affords relief, but is constructive and encouraging. How many people who tell of their troubles promiscuously, do so with a desire to get at the true cause? You are expected to listen, it is hoped you will sympathize; but should you offer anything in the way of constructive criticism, you have over-stepped the mark of minding your own business!

The vulnerability of the self to suggestions pertaining to the body, is well illustrated in the patent medicine business. It has been proved over and over again that an inert substance like flour or milk-sugar, in pill form, and supported by suggestive advertisements, will find an excellent market in a very short time. Year after year all kinds of fakirs, aided by auto-suggestion on the part of the public, take in millions of dollars, largely by suggesting an ailment, and then selling the remedy to cure it. Judging by photographic displays in almanacs, apparently in many instances the suggestion of disease and of cure works equally well in both directions.

The noted French neurologist, Dr. Paul Dubois,* in order to test the suggestibility of his nervous patients, allowed a co-worker to take each patient into a room where an electrical apparatus was set up on a table. There extended from a rheostat, two wires to which brass rings were attached. The patient was requested to place these on his fingers. The operator took his place beside the apparatus, and turned the switch, simply asking the patient to describe what he felt. Inch by inch he would move the coil as if to make the current stronger. Of a large number of patients so treated, over two-thirds of them "complained of various sensations of pricking, warmth, or burning, and took pleasure in describing them minutely." The apparatus was in no way connected with a battery, and was quite without power to produce sensation.

Was the sensation real? Most certainly it was. It did not come from the battery, however, any more than your rapid heart, weakness, and perspiration, came from a burglar. It came from a suggested idea which, from your knowledge of nerve

* Dr. Paul Dubois—"The Psychic Treatment of Nervous Disorders," Funk and Wagnalls Co., 1906.

paths, you must realize was itself the result of an impulse stimulating psycho-physical processes. If into motor nerves, a thought or suggestion can send impulses strong enough to activate the muscles of the stomach to emesis, it also can send into sensory nerves, impulses strong enough to produce feeling.

When the moral self makes a practise of questioning the truth in a suggestion, it is unlikely that obvious untruth will be entertained or allowed to perpetrate an evil effect on the body for more than a very short time. Where, however, the feeling and the desire produced by each sensation is acted upon without question, untrue suggestion is very liable to become organized into untrue belief which gathers force, until, in the form of an obsession, it usurps the moral self and takes possession of conduct.

Let us consider a case which illustrates the effects of untrue suggestion on a prevalent type of poorly controlled intellect. A young lady is an only child in a family of good standing. There is little remarkable in her personal history; outside of the ordinary childhood disabilities, she has never been very ill. She usually experienced difficulty, however, in making her grades at a private school. When she was a little girl, an uncle, who lived with the family, had frequent attacks and died of angina pectoris. At the time of our narrative, however, the young lady has almost forgotten that she ever had an uncle. Her father is a hard working and prosperous business man. Her mother has never been considered very strong, and prefers complacently to gratify her daughter's wishes rather than spend the energy necessary to try to teach her discrimination and self-control. The mother prides herself in the thought that her daughter has been brought up very carefully, and that she is as innocent as a babe in her knowledge of the ways of the wicked world. Except for an occasional upheaval when "Father puts his foot down," and the inevitable little tiffs with mother, when she is not feeling up to going to places, life for the daughter is carefully protected, and is more or less a dreamy anticipation of pleasure.

One evening the daughter discovers that she has been jilted by a young man who professed to love her more than life itself. Days upon days of weeping ensue. She cannot eat; she *will* not eat. She will see none of her friends. Her mother and father are torn by sympathy (which, by the way, is not an unmixed blessing) and do their best to console her with kind words, flowers, and other little attentions. They observe what they consider to be a discreet silence on the love tragedy, but remark on her pallor and loss of weight, and are unable to keep back the tears when they hear her say she wishes she could die. By degrees the daughter is induced to go for drives, and finally the father arranges a trip to the seaside for the summer.

At the seaside hotel the young lady spends much

of her time thinking of herself and of her troubles, and in reading cheap novels. She would feel ashamed to talk about the cause of her trouble, so she suppresses that, but she finds an outlet for her emotions in sighing, evincing great depression and tiredness, and sub-consciously begging sympathy through her actions.

One night as she lies awake thinking of her wounded feelings, she suddenly becomes aware that she can hear her heart beating. She has read in novels of the heroine, deserted by a base lover, dying of heart trouble, and a cold shiver passes through her spine. Finally she manages to overcome the auto-suggestion, and drops asleep, but in the morning she looks long and carefully in the mirror to see if there be anything in her face suggestive of heart trouble.

Some days later, on the beach she happens to hear an old lady telling a friend all about the trouble she has had with her heart ever since she ate cucumbers without first soaking them in salt water. The young lady joins the group, and very sympathetically and earnestly inquires about the elder lady's many and manifold symptoms. Day by day she develops a more absorbing interest in her own body, and a larger repertoire of symptoms. She notices that at times her heart beats faster, and at others nearly stops. It is suggested to her that eating meat increases the blood pressure, so she discontinues eating meat. She has heard of people dropping dead through running for a street car, and so curtails her exercise to gentle ambulations. As the majority of people are somewhat disposed to ridicule her assertions with regard to heart weakness, unless she finds somebody who is really sympathetic, she discreetly gives up talking about her trouble.

The following winter, feeling more than usually well, she is induced to attend a large dinner and theatre party. She partakes of an unusually hearty meal, for it is beautifully served, and later with more abandon of spirit than she has experienced for many months, she drives to the theatre. At the end of the first act, when everybody is talking and laughing, she feels her attention drawn to some one in the audience who is looking at her. Her eyes meet those of her untrue lover, who sits beside *his wife.* For a moment the blood surges to her face and then ebbs, leaving her pale and weak. Somebody asks, "What's the matter?" She replies, "I must go home; I am ill."

She goes quietly to bed. Her mouth is too dry to talk, and her head is aching violently. Hours of excitement pass away, and, as she tosses, she becomes increasingly uncomfortable. With a change in position, the gas which has accumulated from the contents of arrested digestion, suddenly presses upward on the diaphragm, and embarrasses her breathing. A sharp pain seizes her under the left breast. With a shriek she jumps up in bed and calls out wildly—"Father, mother, my heart, oh, my God!" The terrified parents rush to their daughter's room to find her clutching at her heart, rocking forward and backward in bed, her face livid and pinched, eyes staring from their sockets, lips blue, and beads of perspiration standing on her forehead.

Ever to be recalled are the seeming hours which preceded the doctor's arrival. At the front door the excited father calls to the approaching physician, "Oh, doctor, hurry please; my daughter is dying!" In two moments the doctor is at the bedside. Having given considerable attention to "nerves," he is able quickly to take in the simulated condition. He knows that young ladies very rarely suffer from angina pectoris, that the attack practically never occurs during the resting hours, and that the real condition differs in some important respects from the pseudo. To leave no shadow of doubt, however, he makes a careful examination, and, while proceeding to administer a simple carminative and sedative, he relieves the situation by saying: "There is nothing organically wrong; it is only 'nerves!'"

XII

SUPPRESSION AND DISSOCIATION

IT is quite evident that impulses which course through nerve paths in the brain, travel on different days, and on different hours of the same day, with varying degrees of facility. We all experience times when our thoughts scintillate as it were, with the vividness of sunbeams dancing on waves—when we realize we are at our best. We all experience other times when, use our volition as we will, we are stupid and thick-headed; and we know it.

Among psychologists much discussion of late has centered on this state of affairs, as well as on its perverted results, to arrive if possible at an adequate understanding of the physiological state in the brain corresponding to the mental condition. Thus far it has proved impossible to examine the brain cells of a conscious person under the microscope, and so actually to see what takes place. There is much to support the theory, however, that either in themselves some brain cells possess the power of drawing in their short antennæ, thus causing a gap at their junction with other cells; or that some other factor operates to cause a dissociation of one cell from the other. In any event, the synapses or nerve centres of many nerve paths appear to become at times so resistant to the passage of impulses that something analagous to a breach of contact takes place.

As the beneficent hand of sleep is laid softly upon us, it would seem that, one by one, the association nerve cells of the brain gently retract their galvanic arms. The breaks thus formed in the energy paths cannot be spanned by impulses which otherwise would give rise to thoughts. Gradually the process of dissociation extends to the sensory nerve paths of the brain; the noises of the night fall on unhearing ears, and the marauding mosquito is free to partake of an uninterrupted meal from the heavy and insensible sleeper. The motor paths to some extent, are also affected, as is evidenced by our uncertain gait when aroused suddenly from heavy slumber by some alarm.

On the other hand, when impulses actively course through nerve paths, the contact appears to become closer, the synapses seem to limber up, and allow the current to pass more easily. Sometimes when we have mental steam up, it is difficult to slow down. Following an evening's excitement, it is a common experience to lie awake, while, quite against our wishes, thoughts of all that has happened or has been said, continue to arrest our attention, and withhold us from "the city of sleep." Even as, one by one, the lights of the mind go out, impulses of subjective origin continue to activate some memory systems, and through an ever-deepening haze, grotesque figures masquerade in the dim light of a nearly extinguished consciousness.

Again, in the early morning hours, as the interrupted transmitters of life one by one resume their function of illumination, impulses of innate longings, which continuously have been denied expression, finding an unguarded path, are the first to get through the synapses, and give rise to dreams of extraordinary and complex pageantry.

Psychiatry makes it clear that in the dream, as in the ravings of a lunatic, there is method in the madness, and that by means of a distorted symbolic imagery, the secret wishes of the subconscious mind are revealed. In many instances, in the dream there can be found a suppressed wish which, unrealized by the dreamer, is having an unfortunate influence over his life, and is tormenting his soul.

In addition to the natural physiological process of dissociation and reassociation of energy paths, there is the artificial condition produced by certain drugs. For example, the anæsthetic effects of chloroform and ether are well known, and the blessed relief from pain afforded by morphine testifies to a blocking of impulses in sensory nerve paths. There are other drugs which have just the opposite action, as is recognized by the effects of strong coffee, and such excitants as alcohol and strychnine.

Acting like drugs, certain mental activities and

inactivities possess the power, on the one hand, of blocking impulses in the brain, and, on the other of facilitating their passage. In his " Psychopathology of Every Day Life," Professor Sigmund Freud has shown by many interesting examples that sudden forgetting about things we know perfectly well, as for example the names of people, the numbers of houses, the titles of books, and so on, is brought about by some unpleasant association, quite possibly forgotten or unrecognized, which causes *mental suppression.* On the other hand, there are thoughts of an uplifting, invigorating nature, such, for example, as thoughts which afford encouragement. These facilitate the flow of nervous impulses, and thereby enable us to unlock potential energies, and go forward with increased efficiency.

Mental suppression may vary from a trivial holding back of our natural ebullition, to a fearsome and agonized forcing under of a something in our minds—a something the existence of which, even to ourselves, we will not admit—a something which haunts and hurts.

People in general have a poor understanding of the difference between suppression and self-control. Supposing themselves to be exercising self-control, when they wish to do an unwise thing, metaphorically speaking, they sit upon themselves. When a master sentiment for truth is lacking, this is more or less inevitable. Unless one has the firm conviction that always, under every circumstance, the wise thing is the most advantageous thing, of course the wish to do what is unwise will wait around and argue its case, while the moral self must constantly suppress it to prevent its going into action.

When one wish to do what is wise reigns supreme, all other wishes fall into line or are given up. They are not suppressed, because that would mean that they were still alive and active, but held under. Suppression ensues because the moral self has not learned the art of letting go, of renouncing. The wish, in spite of its unwisdom, continues to be entertained, and the constant effort required to hold it in check consumes considerable energy.

To varying extents, everybody suffers from suppression. We all recognize ourselves in Theodore Martin's lines:

> "Within my earthly temple there's a crowd;
> There's one of us that's humble, one that's proud,
> There's one that's broken-hearted for his sins,
> There's one that unrepentant sits and grins;
> There's one that loves his neighbor as himself,
> And one that cares for naught but fame and pelf.
> From much corroding care I should be free
> If I could once determine which is me."

If we could develop a sufficiently powerful master sentiment for truth, there would be no difficulty in determining "which is me." There would be no divided interests. The moral self would have each part of the mind pulling in the same direction, namely the direction of truth, as closely as it can be conceived.

In your mind is the reservation that this would be all right, provided, in each instance, you understood just what was the truth. In your case, life is so complex that the greatest difficulty appears to be the finding of the truth. Whenever you are in a state of indecision as to which of two courses to follow, the indecision arises either from lack of knowledge or, more likely, from a mental conflict. Where the indecision is due only to lack of knowledge, there is perfect willingness and desire to follow *either* course, just so long as it can be shown to be the wiser. Under such circumstances no mental conflict can take place, there can be no suppression of one interest which wishes to usurp. Such a state of mind is healthy, and stimulates a search for truth. In matters of every day concern, the true course to follow can easily be arrived at by consulting the right authorities.

When there is indecision due to desire in a questionable direction, worry is sure to follow. Worry is nothing but mental conflict, and fear of not getting one's own way. Here there is lacking the genuine desire to follow whatever be true. There is even unwillingness to abide by an authority other than one's self. There is quick resistance to any suggestion which threatens the desire. The selfish interest prefers to shove through the matter without consideration, for fear, if reason be applied, it may interfere with personal gratification. It is the *being unwilling to* be wise which causes the trouble.

When suppression becomes a habit, and it is the rule to suppress instead of to give up a wish, it is not surprising that fatigue, unwarranted by one's activities, should show itself. Two kinds of striving are going on. The unwise wish is striving for expression, and the moral self is striving to suppress the wish. There is a constant conflict in the mind, a working to cross purposes, with the natural confusion and instability which conflict always brings. The vacillation of worry ensues; one moment something favours the suppressed wish, the next minute something else makes the perpetration of the wish appear too risky. In all probability the vacillation is punctuated with procrastination; the controversy being unpleasant, the wish is allowed to rest until some new stimulus renews the mental conflict. Impatience and irritability are counterparts to the confusion and self-dissatisfaction. Discouragement, depression and all kinds of apprehension make their appearance. In the brain, the drug-like effects of mild suppression are demonstrated in sudden forgetfulness of well-known data, absent-mindedness, difficulty in concentration, foggy consciousness, and inefficiency.

The imprisonment of energy, as the result of suppression, is shown in the remarkable change in activity which takes place, once there enters a factor which diverts the attention and suddenly reverses the emotional tone from a depressive character to one which is invigorating. For example, feeling "dog-tired" and perhaps ill, along comes a much desired invitation holding promise of a good time, and extended with the correct fillip of enthusiasm and persuasion. Literally a waking-up process immediately takes place; through re-associated energy paths there is forthwith established a gangway to the energy hitherto pent up in the brain, and the fun is enjoyed zealously by the previously tired person.

The best teachers of little children well realize the dour effect of rough methods in education, as contrasted with the assistance afforded the child's perception by enthusiasm and encouragement. With the understanding of psychological principles professed by German scientists, it is surprising that in the late war they permitted the deliberate development of hate in the minds of the German soldiery. Even in war, hate is a paralyzing passion. Men can find more energy in martial music and in patriotic enthusiasm than in hymns of hate or curses.

Most nervous people will sacrifice much in order to preserve peace and avoid trouble. Their wish to avoid pain, even the discomfort of volition, is their greatest undoing. Often they have thoughts the expression of which they know would occasion an unpleasant discussion, so they take the line of least resistance, and suppress their thoughts. Nevertheless, they continue to feel the influence of the thought, and suffer the effects of suppression.

You ask: "Is it better to keep quiet, or have a verbal encounter?" That depends entirely on the truth contained in the thought. The impulsive blurting-out of unconsidered criticisms is undoubtedly responsible for the majority of family bickerings, and, as a rule, such criticism is simply an emotional reaction to something which has touched one's special interests. On the other hand, to hear truth worsted, and not to defend it, is moral cowardice.

There are two ways to give expression to thought; the way of feeling and the way of reason; the impulsive way or the carefully considered way. The suppressed thought is, as a rule, not only unexpressed, it is unconsidered, unanalyzed, and is stored in the capital stock of the mind in its crude state. Subjected to analysis, very often it would appear ridiculous, and would be afforded a hurried exit.

Of all thoughts those relating to sexual matters are probably the most susceptible of suppression. For obvious reasons, they do not permit of free discussion, and unfortunately, in many instances, there is lacking the reasoning knowledge to give to them subjective consideration. People who have been brought up under moral influences which are prudish—people of the type which regards it as a sin to allow the mind to consider anything of a sexual nature—are able to adapt themselves but poorly to thoughts or suggestion of immoral import.

A woman, for example, who does not make a practice of using her reason, is liable to fall a prey to the suggestion that her husband is unfaithful. If she has been brought up in a prudish environment, the suggestion assumes an awfulness which not only renders its discussion unthought of, but prohibits its consideration by herself. Quite probably, if the suggestion were analyzed, it would prove ridiculous, but it is suppressed as a thought which is unworthy, unjust, and untrue. Although the thought be too sordid to be admitted to consciousness, it produces its full quota of feeling, and influences conduct, whenever it is stimulated by something associated with it. It prompts its victim to assure her friends of the virtues of her husband, and to build all sorts of sad defences against the inroads on her confidence. It will bring on also sudden and unaccountable feelings of faintness, equally sudden attacks of weeping, and withal, exaggerated attempts to be helpful and affectionate. As a result of the suppression, the dissociation of energy paths may reveal itself in surprising forgetfulness, absence of mind, and even a state of going about as though in a dream.

In a case of this kind, it does not require much in the way of psycho-analysis to discover the complex which is causing symptoms of both body and mind.

The reactions are so very obvious that, even if the woman herself is unable to appreciate where the trouble lies, the husband in time suspects the cause. He in turn reacts; either he adds fuel to the fire, by becoming embarrassed, or, if he be of a cheap sort, he takes a devilish delight in assisting his wife to become a nervous invalid.

On the other hand, if the husband be of the type who acts, instead of reacts, he takes chances on an unpleasant seance, and carefully getting rid of any *feeling* in the matter, exposes her suppressed thoughts to the light of his wife's consciousness. His wife, of course, weeps, and assails vehemently what she avers is an unfair insinuation. Such a thought has never entered her mind, etc., etc., but the sunny care-free days which follow, point to a release from bondage, and are strong evidence that the mind has been purged of an undigested and irritable ingredient.

Some men would consider such action on the part of a husband a sign of weakness. If it be weakness to bring the light of truth into a poor sick mind, if it be weakness to break the bonds of a suffering soul, where do we find strength? Is it in a false pride which disdains what is uncomplimentary or in the uncompromising superiority that would leave a sick mind to suffer? Strength lies not in might but in right. Personal power does not pose on a pedestal; it stoops to conquer.

XIII

THE MAJOR NERVOUS DISABILITIES

EXCESSIVE and abnormal dissociation is caused not only by suppression of thoughts and feelings, but by any considerable shock or strongly depressive emotion. It is as though nature realized that too much emotional excitement existed in the nervous organism, and, in order to cut off part of the energy, applied a non-conductor through dissociation of some of the energy paths.

Text books on "nerves" (the functional neuroses) mention *shock* as an important factor in causation. We refer not to surgical shock, but to spiritual or mental shock. Surgical shock is a condition which results from body injury; it presents definite physical signs, is little affected by the personality, and is a matter rather of hours than weeks. Surgical shock is likely, of course, to cause mental shock as well, but mental shock may be, and generally is, quite independent of organic injury. For example, the young lady referred to in the train wreck showed no physical hurt, but received a severe mental shock; the young lady who was jilted by her lover also received a mental shock, differing only in degree, not in kind.

Shock undoubtedly *appears* to be the starting

place of much nervousness, but why the shock? The young lady sitting in the next seat to our nervous victim of the train wreck undergoes identically the same terrifying experience; to her, however, the adventure remains but an incident. Similarly, a few of the finest girls in the land have been jilted by some Beau Brummel, but the experience has left them only a little more worldly wise.

Two mothers receive word from the War Office that their sons have been killed. Each loves her boy as only a mother can. One goes utterly to pieces—nervous prostration, nurses, whispered inquiries, and all the rest of it. The second—we respect too greatly the dignity of her quiet self-control even to discuss it.

Two husbands receive word from the Stock Exchange that their fortunes have gone up in smoke. The one goes home and blows out his brains, or maybe he has the decency to do it somewhere else. The other says to his wife, "Well, old girl, it is up to us to camp out in the back yard;" and his wife realizes that there will be happiness in so doing.

What a life history is revealed in individual acts! The art of self-control is not a life preserver which can be left in a small compartment, to be called into service only when the frail bark ships a heavy sea. If we would weather the shocks of life's voyage, we must be seasoned, to the extent, at least, of not being upset by squalls and adverse currents.

It is human to suffer from spiritual shock, and there are none of us who become so expert in adaptation to the unhappy surprises of existence but that, at times, we are overwhelmed by feeling. The point of importance is, the amount of capital stock in equilibrium we store up by refusing to be disappointed over little things. We should lay firm hold on the truth expressed in the lines:

> " Oh, a trouble's a ton, or a trouble's an ounce,
> Or a trouble is what you make it,
> And it isn't the fact that you're hurt that counts,
> But only how did you take it."

Everything depends on how active the moral self is to-day, to-morrow, and every day, in letting go, in non-resisting, in achieving the attitude of, " Oh, well, I am willing! " instead of being disappointed when a wish is not gratified. After all, there is nothing in life that is of such desperate importance that it cannot be given up. Even life itself, if one will stop to reflect, is important only in proportion to its productiveness.

The seeming importance of anything is entirely relative to the strength of the wish concerning it. Take away the wish for it, and what does it amount to? The function of the moral self is to control the wish, and to prevent it from assuming such proportions that it not only appears to be more important than truth itself, but becomes prepared to trample on other people's rights, and even the rights of the wisher's own body, in order to gratify its selfishness.

Be it conceded that shock and disappointment are important factors in upsetting the body functions, especially the normal working of the mind. At the same time let us realize fully that shock and disappointment are proportional to the frailties of the moral self, and occur only because the moral self is not an artist in its work of self-control or renunciation.

That fatigue, aside from tiredness brought on through worry, can cause dissociation with mental disturbance, was well demonstrated in a six-day bicycle race at Madison Square Garden some years ago. Toward the end of the race, the riders became seized with delusions and hallucinations. They imagined that people were seeking to interfere with them, and went out of their course in order to avoid imaginary obstacles. With fatigue states, however, as with other causes of nervousness, we should ask, why the excessive fatigue? Is the moral self permitting the body to do what is irrational? To be sure, it may *appear* at the time to be worth while, but, no matter what it appears, it does not as a fact pay in the long run.

Through causing an upset in the normal distribution of energy, dissociation not only occasions clouding of the intellect and interference with rational thinking and feeling, but plays an important part in bringing about perverted action of the stomach, heart, and other organs. In their turn these symptoms cause more depressive emotions. In this way, uncontrolled feelings cause a vicious circle of reactions, each egging the other on.

As a result of the more accentuated forms of dissociation, dark moods may occur, in which strongly depressive emotions overwhelm consciousness, and, for the time being, alter the whole personality. When the mood is colouring everything in life with sombre tones, some kind friend, as in the case of King Saul, might play on a harp, or seek in other ways to disperse the saddening gloom. For all his generous-hearted endeavours, however, he is just as likely as David of old, to meet with verbal javelins as with thanks. While under its influence, the victim of the mood may realize that he is acting to very poor advantage, but he is not sufficiently practised in making moral effort to enable him to rise above the shadow of the emotional cloud. In such cases, the dissociation and its effects, though marked, are nevertheless of the more or less transitory nature common to the forms already discussed.

Of greater seriousness are the more permanent conditions, where large areas of the brain suddenly become dissociated from their paths of communication, and the memories of years become an utter blank. The interesting conditions of trance, somnambulance, and dual personality, are likewise to be explained by abnormal dissociation of this character.

There are many other more or less fixed conditions, where the dissociation does not include such a large brain area, and where just a few memory systems (co-conscious ideas they are called) while still in touch with the emotional centres, become separated from the control of consciousness, and stage a little tragedy on their own account. The hysterical crisis, where, quite obviously, there is a waking dream perpetrating its nightmare effect on consciousness, is a case in point.

A beneficent function of the psycho-therapeutist is to find dissociated thoughts by means of psycho-analysis, and through making them clear to the patient's perception, to reassociate them with the main consciousness. In other words, the individual is brought to realize that the waking dream *is a dream.* Sometimes months of painstaking effort are required to find the lost and recalcitrant fragments of personality. As one by one they are discovered, the patient is subject to emotional outbursts, but later, we "see him that was possessed with a devil, and had the legion, (of personalities) sitting, and clothed, and in his right mind." *

In some cases, the more serious dissociations do not remain confined to the higher systems which

* St. Mark v, 15.

represent memories, or perceptions, and which, as we have seen, play a large part in thought. They involve systems lower in the hierarchy as well, with the result that both sensation and muscular movement may be cut off. Thus, following some highly emotional experience, such a dissociation may cause for an indefinite period, loss of sensation in some part of the body, and inability to move that part. It is possible, also, that wasting of the tissues may occur in consequence of the inactivity. That this state of affairs is due to perverted action on the part of the synapses or nerve centres, and is in no way organic, is proved by the fact that, in a hypnotized subject, the condition can be produced or removed at the suggestion of the operator.

It is through apparently marvellous recovery in cases such as these that the greatest impetus is afforded to so-called faith-healing. As we have explained, suggestions causing invigorating emotions may have beneficent association effect, just as circumstances affording depressive emotions may have an unfortunate dissociation action. So it is that, under strong inspirational persuasion, the lines of communication may become re-established, and, as a result, the dumb are made to speak, the blind are enabled to see, and the palsied take up their beds and walk.

Just what part perverted dissociation might play in the cause and aggravation of organic disease, has not been seriously enough considered. It is conceivable that *in some cases* it might exercise a profound influence.

From Chapter III it will be recalled that a passing fancy, or thought, and a sentiment or belief, differ as widely as do a sheet of paper and a book. The former is psychical in character, and is wafted hither and thither by every wind that blows; the latter, while open to influence by a passing current, is more or less deeply impressed in nerve synapses, and can be dislodged only by means of considerable energy. A belief may evolve gradually through means of an oft-repeated suggestion, and thoughts which render it plausible, or it may be built up impulsively, as the product of an intense emotional experience. Whichever way it be formed, once it becomes an organized system it is not to be banished with a mere " Pshaw! " or " Fiddlesticks! " It is there for good or ill, to be made stronger by becoming attached to kindred beliefs which support it, or to become weaker through the organization of sentiments which are opposed to and neutralize it.

It will be recalled that memory or belief systems (perceptual systems) which are in association areas of the brain, are linked up in the motor area with energy paths going to the muscles. This is essential in order that we should act from memory. In the same way some memory systems are associated with energy paths going to glands, as can be demonstrated in yourself by conjuring up memories connected with the body's appetites. For example, you can stimulate the salivary glands by thinking of, or seeing, some particularly enticing kind of food.

This is all very good, so long as the memory which influences belief and action is based on truth. Through repeated inculcation of false suggestion, however, and the organization of fixed false beliefs, some strange things happen. Activity in different organs of the body, with secretion on the part of glands, may become responsive to a belief in what is *untrue,* in identically the same way as when the belief is based on truth. If the belief be based on memories of what is true, the body actions and feelings, brought about through the connections established with the belief, are serviceable, and help to adapt a person to his environment. If the belief be untrue, the feelings and effects which result are disabling, and are such as to misadapt one to his environment.

A most common instance of a misadapting complex arising through false suggestion is found in certain cases of hay fever. At the sight of roses, or golden rod, many people promptly develop a congestion of the nasal mucous membrane, with sneezing, watering of the eyes, and profuse nasal secretion. It makes no difference whether the roses be artificial; if the belief, quite possibly subconscious, be that the roses are of the "hay fever kind," the attack is forthcoming. Instead of the belief being related to roses, it may be another fixed idea, such as the " last week of June," which brings into effect the conjured up anticipation.

Through emotional stress rather than through dispassionate education, a fixed idea may become linked up with sensory nerves which produce pain. The victim is quite unaware of the cause, but whenever any associated idea stimulates the complex, painful sensations are the result. The pain or neurosis is felt in the arm, leg, or whatever part of the anatomy is supplied by the sensory nerve involved. So it is that some organized thoughts are like a thorn in the flesh, and will not be removed until the complex is found by the psycho-analyst, and truth is applied to it in sufficient measure to render it powerless.

There is not a body function which may not be perverted through the malevolent influence of a false and fixed belief. In this way we get diarrhœa, constipation, chronic indigestion, greatly exaggerated functioning on the part of the kidneys, all sorts of heart action, nervous cough, insomnia, periodical headaches, and pseudo-representations of every pathological condition known to the public.

It is not to be imagined that the sufferer, in any sense of the word, is malingering. In the first place, there may have been a wish in the matter which favoured the suggestion taking hold. Long since, however, the suggestion, no matter in what way it originated, has become an organized belief.

To be sure, the patient will freely admit that the whole thing has a sense of unreality, but he is true to his false belief, and it is as foolish to find fault with him for his symptoms, as it would be to accuse yourself of false fear with reference to a man whom you *knew* wished to assassinate you.

It will be readily realized that all muscular movement, from the handling of a jack-knife to the most elaborate technique in piano-playing, depends for its successful execution on the formation by education of organized associations between the material elements of memory and those of action; further, that a great degree of independent action or automatism may be acquired by many of these normal complexes. For example, many a person can engage in a conversation, whilst, almost independent of his attention, his nerve centres enable his hands to carry out the technique of piano-playing. Again, many a woman can knit a stocking and read a story at the same time.

Instead of some useful action, like piano-playing, knitting, or any of the artful manipulations, there may develop complexes the stimulation of which bring about muscular contractions that are anything but serviceable. In children especially. unserviceable muscular movements may arise as a result of imitation, and may, through frequent repetition, become habitual and automatic. In view, however, of our being able to control our voluntary muscles with an effort of the will, it usually requires in adults impulses of considerable emotional energy, suddenly to create abnormal complexes, the later stimulation of which occasion annoying automatic muscular movements. The peculiar grimaces and habitual twitches of the facial muscles are evidence of disadvantageous complexes of this kind. Of similar origin are muscular compulsions of the arm or leg which are both painful to watch, and embarrassing to the victim.

The origin of such muscular movements in adults is nearly always staged in great emotional stress of one kind or another. As illustrated in our victim of the railway accident, the muscular compulsion may date from some occasion when great emotional energy would seem, as it were, to have blazed a trail through nerve synapses with irrational ferocity. In this way an open and perverted path is left for nervous energy, which, for indefinite periods, permits the misadapting muscular movements above described.

Finally, there are cases in which there may be both marked dissociation and complexes causing perverted actions of all kinds. The resolutely suppressed memory, finding no other avenue for its strong emotional energy, would seem to burrow false paths, and bring about perverted associations which are among the most difficult to rectify. The unhappy memories may have had their origin in childhood, and, through suppression, have long since become lost to waking consciousness. In the night time, these offspring of a well-intentioned but untrue and cruel moral teaching, cry aloud from the sepulchres of the mind, and, temporarily breaking their bondage, disturb the sweet peacefulness of sleep with their ghoulish pantomines and terrifying representations. Indeed, they may overstep the confines of the night, and trail hallucinatory ravings into waking thoughts.

Such is the power of untruth that although taught with the kindest intentions imaginable, as is usually the case, it may cause such irrational magnifying of wrongdoing, such suffering for supposedly unpardonable sin, such violent suppression of thought, as for example in the memory of some trivial immorality of childhood, that, without the healing hand of science, the victim is doomed to wander as a morbidly shy, self-condemned, inwardly despised, and outwardly dejected, human wreck.

The stronger the belief in untrue ideas, the more virulent is their effect. The less there is of reasoning, the more easily does untruth take hold. Good intention, or the craving for sympathy in opinion, is not enough. Upon all entrusted with moral education there is a responsibility either to base their teaching on truth as it is revealed in fact, or to make it clear that there is difference of opinion which ought to be respected. Is the truth with regard to anything so well established that one interpretation of it is absolute and immortal? Can any of us afford to have our beliefs become so fixed that they cannot be altered or enlarged through a fuller revelation of truth?

PART III

FACTS APPLIED

XIV

THE OBJECT IN VIEW

HAVING shown in earlier chapters how it is that symptoms of nervousness owe their origin to failure of the moral self to make the body conform to natural law, we are now in a position to indicate the application of these principles to living, and to give you through definite directions an opportunity to regain health and happiness, and to develop personal power.

Had you understood, long ago, all about the cause of " nerves," you probably might have saved yourself much suffering. The simple fact is, however, that nervous symptoms have troubled you at greater or lesser intervals for some time, and now your problem is, not so much to account for the nervousness, as to determine how to overcome it.

Recovery from nervous symptoms presents little difficulty, and will come about in anywhere from a few days to a few weeks, if you will follow directions faithfully. Recovery from symptoms, however, is only a small part of the cure. The moral self has only to make some improvement in volition and control for the symptoms to disappear. Without continued exercise of the self, however, the symptoms are liable to return.

There are all kinds of remedial measures which might be applied to relieve symptoms temporarily. Isolation, rest cures, trips to the seaside, hydrotherapy, electricity, nerve tonics, and many other means, good in themselves, may remedy the immediate cause of the suffering, but they fail in lasting benefit. After a storm, we may use pumps and other means to relieve the flooded and denuded country, but unless we set to work systematically to build a dyke, the next storm may send the devastating waves just where they went before. In the same way, we may employ many means of bringing relief to a nervously prostrated body, but it is a mistake to suppose that such measures can stem the flood of the next storm. If we would attain radical relief, we must devote our attention to storm-proof stamina, rather than to means which, too often, render us dependent instead of making us masters of the situation.

Do not infer that isolation, rest, and other measures are not necessary in many cases. Indeed, some patients could never secure a start along the right road without being freed temporarily of conditions which handicap their progress. The time should come, and come quickly, however, when a patient should cease running away, should face his environment fearlessly, and should apply what he has learned about the art of adaptation.

When he has reached this point, he is ready to do away with palliative measures, and to study the radical cure of nervousness as outlined in this book.

The radical cure of "nerves" is no more difficult, and no less difficult, than changing a habit. You perhaps have been told about your illness that all you need to do is to "go home and forget it." If you regard the matter in any such trivial manner, your cure, to say the least, will take a somewhat prolonged period. On the other hand, the length of time required for a complete recovery depends on the fixity of the habit you have to change, and on the earnestness of your desire to grapple with it.

There are many people who, much as they complain of their nervous symptoms, do not consider it worth while to forego the self-indulgence which holds them in bondage; in other words, they consider the treatment more unpleasant than the complaint. Such cases have not gone far enough in experiencing the unhappy and painful consequences of their nervousness, to develop the strong wish that some day will be theirs—the wish to sacrifice anything and everything on earth in order to find peace of mind and body.

Those who have the true wish to rise above their weakness can rest assured that earnestness is all that is necessary to bring success. Each day the work of changing the habit will become easier. What is regarded to-day as a deprivation and a bore will, in but a short time, afford such a carefree feeling that the exercise of volition will be found to more than pay in actual joy of living.

Let us go right to the heart of the matter. There is just one habit which has to be changed, the habit of acting on fancy instead of on fact, the habit of allowing yourself to be ruled by suggestion instead of by truth. Since you have begun to experience unpleasant results from this habit, you have been concentrating all your attention, not on the habit, but on its unpleasant results, and, very naturally, you have intensified these through the increased attention given them. To be sure, you have been saying, "I shall not think this untrue thought, this pain is not real, this apprehension is imaginary," and so on, but by so doing you have been culturing the thought, accentuating the pain, and developing the apprehension.

It is folly to suppose that you can develop self-control in one small department of your life, namely, with regard to symptoms or those things which cause you unpleasantness, and give yourself a free rein in all other matters. Self-control is an art—the art of giving up an unwise impulse. You feel you would like to be able to give up or control your strongly emotional impulses when they impel you to act irrationally, but what about your ordinary every-day mild emotions which only *prompt* you to do what is unwise? Can you control them? *Do* you control them?

If you wish to learn self-control, start in with

your every-day comparatively unemotional, unwise wishes. Acquire the stamina to control them, and soon you will come to the place where you can control the strong emotions sufficiently to prevent the occurrence of body symptoms. Before long you will go further, and develop the personal power which for ever will put an end to nervous weakness.

As in self-control, likewise in the matter of volition; you wish you had the nervous strength to overcome certain obstacles which particularly afford you inconvenience and unpleasantness. For example, you would like to take your part in the reading of an original paper before the social club of which you are a member, but you are lacking in the stuff to put the enterprise through. Have you thought of the damage to your volition that arises through giving in each day to your lethargic feelings? It is folly to suppose that you can run away from ninety-five per cent. of the hard things in life, and successfully challenge the remaining five per cent.

So it is that your treatment involves a change in policy in your *general* living. It requires a finding out of what is the true course to follow right down the line, because everything you do, and more particularly the things you fail to do, have an important bearing on health and well-being. On the one hand, there are a lot of " I don't wants " which have to be overridden with volition, and acted upon in spite of feelings to the contrary, and, on the other hand, there are a series of " I wants " which have to be given up. Strange as it may seem, your symptoms are the black sheep of the unwise " I want " group, and, just like the unwise wishes, they cannot be given up by thinking about them and acting on account of them.

The more you potter over your symptoms, the more intense they will become, but the more, as it were, you come up behind your symptoms with stamina acquired in a broader field, the more quickly they will vanish of their own accord. The necessary requirement is to leave your symptoms strictly alone, and to develop your stamina on something which you can master, something which is not involved in impulses too strong for your moral self.

If you are to make progress, one understanding is necessary; the fact that a course of action is true, right, reasonable, and rational, is to constitute grounds all-sufficient for you to follow it, no matter what your wishes or feelings may be to the contrary. In other words, you must be willing to give up your unwise wishes, and to put into action that which is wise. " But," you exclaim, " this is what I have been *trying* to do all my life! " You have with just one reservation, and that is that you are to be the authority to determine what for you is wise.

Your wishes with regard to things in general lean to the side of feeling, and therefore colour your conception of what is wise. You are perfectly law-abiding, as far as the laws of man and the Church are concerned. Quite possibly you are more God-fearing than the average person, because in this direction your feeling is strong. In the past, however, you have not included wisdom and unwisdom in your tenets of right and wrong. As long as what you have wished has escaped being the old-fashioned "wrong," you have failed to see any important reason why you should not carry it out; hence the "nerves."

One of your characteristics is that you have very strong desires, likes, and dislikes. When you have wished a thing, you have wished it so very much that its perpetration was not to be thwarted merely by the knowledge that it was not wise. As long as it was considered "the thing to do" by the society with which you associate, you hardly deemed it necessary to submit it to kill-joy processes of thought.

This sort of thing, however, cannot go on for any considerable length of time without our discrimination becoming affected along the lines of our wishes. It becomes impossible for us to weigh dispassionately any matter in which a strong wish is wrapped up. The wish not only tends to, but succeeds in influencing our decision.

Quite possibly you may have good judgment with regard to things which are separate from your most loved interests. You can view dispassionately a line of action in which you have no wishes whatever, and probably can estimate correctly what under the circumstances would be wise or unwise. Where, however, you are eager to follow a certain unwise course of conduct, you are in lined to consider it "open to opinion," and will argue, even to yourself, that you are right, notwithstanding that authorities state otherwise.

The fact that you are nervous proves that in everyday affairs you are at war with yourself Although you may argue your intellect into the background, you know intuitively more about what constitutes the true course to be taken than your opposing wishes will permit your muscles to carry out. The trouble is that your wishes have so acquired the habit of suppressing your intellect that you find difficulty in hauling the ungarnished truth into the light of your perception.

Your cure depends on your bringing yourself to look fearlessly and unemotionally at truth, not at your interpretation of truth, but on the cold facts with regard to what comprises true conduct. In your calm reflective moments you will admit that there is but one perfectly true course in any action. The oftener we manage to find the true course, and hold to it, the greater is our personal power. In many matters the facts and recorded experiences which go to prove the best line of action are lacking. In such instances the wise course may be a matter of opinion, or will have to be determined through experience. Nevertheless, in the majority of commonplace habits which influence our lives, what is wise is not a matter of opinion, because facts sufficient to render conclusive the true course have been collected.

We are all disposed to do a great deal of quibbling over this matter of truth-finding. We talk about it as though only the deepest metaphysical problems had to do with it—as though truth were a vague idealistic chant resounding from some organ loft, or an abstract something to be applied with pious sanctity. Many of us act as though we were concerned only about some great spiritual fortune which, in a not very well defined way, is to come to us, and, having our attention fixed on this vision of the future more than on daily living, we neglect to gather from the path we tread, the spiritual ducats on which alone our fortune necessarily depends.

The truth about which we must become vitally concerned, is truth with regard to living, not a post-mortem truth; a concrete truth for action, not an abstract truth for dreaming. With recognized authorities on every branch of this kind of truth at our very doors in public libraries, he who says he cannot find the truth about ordinary living is not looking for it.

Furthermore, if we wish to follow wisdom in any matter which is "open to opinion," we really can prove the wise course to our own satisfaction, and to the satisfaction of any one who differs with us, by being prepared to submit our opinion to the scrutiny of a mutually agreed upon referee, or, for that matter, to anybody and everybody. And why should we refuse to do so?

The impatient voices which raise their protests are from the tyrants of the ancient animal dominion who have been striving to overthrow the intellect. We assert, in the first place, that we do not care to exhibit our private affairs to the scrutiny of an outsider. This is an unreasonable *feeling* which thwarts us in our judgment, and from which none of us entirely escape. It is false pride—the feeling which causes us to resent anybody appearing to know more about what is wise for us than we know ourselves. False pride is but another unwise wish —the wish to *seem* rather than to *be* right, the desire to save appearances at the expense of truth.

In this case reason says to the feeling: "You are based on one of two thoughts—either the knowledge of being wrong which cannot stand exposure, or on the 'holier than thou' thought, which resists a being weighed in the balance by someone else." If we be concerned simply and solely about getting at the truth of the thing, there will be no resistance to consulting another person. Our desire for truth will be a bigger thing than false pride. Furthermore, if we be as much in the right as we declare ourselves to be, to be proved so will afford us satisfaction.

This brings the idea that *we* might be quite willing to follow this plan to arrive at truth, but that the other party to the discussion might perhaps object. While it is always wise to have a regard for other people's wishes, it is other people's responsibility, as well as our own, to get rid of wishes which are unwise. If, in some matter which involves a principle, people insist on taking offence because we intend to have a showdown as to what actually is the truth, we should be perfectly willing for them to do so. Such offence is in reality a compliment; man's character can be judged by the enemies he makes as well as by the friends he has.

> "He never had a friend who never had a foe."

There are still other feelings which combat the idea, and unless you be very much in earnest in this matter, you can easily flim-flam yourself with all sorts of sophistry. You can make a strong appeal to feeling by becoming very sarcastic—the idea presents a rich field for sarcasm and ridicule—forgetting that sarcasm and ridicule prove nothing. This possibility affords the slipperiest spot in all living, and you, and you alone, can supply the sand to enable the wheels of truth to carry you over it.

In addition to false pride, the second great obstacle to open deliberation and fearless facing of truth, is the feeling that in some way your private interests will suffer, that you will have to make sacrifices. There is probably nothing which so much tends to make people doubtful of the value of the literally true course in every-day living as their reluctance to forego pleasure. This is a feature of the situation which has to be faced frankly.

Of the psychical states, pleasure and happiness, you will admit that to be happy is more valuable than to enjoy pleasure. Happiness is dependent on life being lived in accord with true principles, while pleasure can be derived not only from normal healthy activities, but from many intemperate and perverted practises as well. The pleasures which arise from excesses and perversions, however, are death to happiness, because, obviously, they are out of keeping with true principles.

Rational conduct requires a giving-up only of what is harmful to health and happiness. Under these circumstances, is it right to talk about sacrifice, self-denial, and all the rest of it? You continue to have all the pleasure that is not dissipation, and you enjoy it the more on account of its being legitimate, and not disturbing to the mind.

Such a lot of preaching has been to the effect that we should be unselfish, and follow truth from some high and altruistic purpose, that we have lost sight of the fact that in acting wisely there is *the greatest benefit to ourselves,* as well as to others. Conduct which is true can lose nothing of real benefit. It might, in fact, well be defined as that conduct which promotes maximum progress and happiness. Furthermore, no religious faith or philosophy, no matter what its other tenets, is worth anything if it be not based primarily on the belief that to act wisely must inevitably, in this life, work out to our personal advantage. The materialist may not be prepared to admit that this is so, but the psychologist knows it to be a fact, and realizes that the advantage follows immediately on the action.

There is a large group of actions which fall under the classification of asceticism. We should consider carefully all such conduct. A person may undergo real self-denial beyond what, from a moral point of view, is either demanded or expected. If sacrifice of the kind does more good to the world than could have been accomplished in pursuit of ordinary duty, it calls for true admiration. On the other hand, there is nothing to admire in sacrifices which are unwise, sacrifices which diminish one's helpfulness to the world at large. The ascetic young woman, for example, who sacrifices to selfish relatives advantages which on rational grounds should be hers, is acting on unwise feeling, not on a reasoned basis of moral duty to self as well as to others.

Such puritanical teaching as that we should deny ourselves the common sense benefits of living, in order to inherit eternal life, is responsible for many a person coming to the conclusion that he will get out of life all the pleasure possible while the going is good, and take a chance on what is to come later. There may be some excuse for sophistry of the kind where one supposes that virtue consists in cutting oneself off from what is reasonable, or when one does right in order to win favourable comment or reward on the other side of the grave. The egoism underlying such platitudes is apparent, however, when we think in terms of health, efficiency, and ability the better to serve God through service to mankind. Satisfaction and happiness do not come through getting rewards, but through serving.

By following what is true in preference to what you wish, you undoubtedly will have to be ready to give up the immediate satisfaction for a very much larger one which will come later, not after you are dead—although there is reason to suppose you will profit then as well—but in the course of a few weeks. Indeed the very act of making up your mind to this course will loosen the shackles which bind you, and give you your first breath of freedom.

To sum up, your position should be simply this: when you have a wish which conflicts with what according to recognized authorities is wise, you should do your best to drop your wish in the matter, and to follow the true course. You are not going to be dictated to by anybody, but if a difference of opinion arises over anything which involves a principle, you should be ready to abide by the decision of a disinterested and fair-minded authority.

You have no idea what a load such a position will remove from your shoulders—what a release it will be from worse than useless struggling. To take an opposite position is to strive against your own best interests, and to be continually on the *qui vive* for criticism, because you know in your own heart that you are open to criticism. On the other hand, to live in the open, to get rid of all selfish interests, is to say to all comers: "I make mistakes like everybody else, but my chief concern is to follow what is rational. If anybody has a better way of living, I am willing to be shown. I do not promise to act on other people's advice, only on what they can prove to be true."

The object of treatment, then, far from being to deprive you of anything you have had in the past, is aimed at persuading you to give up that which is hurtful to your health, that which is holding you back from fullness of service, in exchange for something which is infinitely less tiring and more satisfying. Treatment aims at bringing mental peace by reinforcing and rendering supreme the wish to follow what is rational. Its purpose is so to adjust your life that through renewed health increased service will become possible, and that the reward of true service—happiness, satisfaction, and freedom—will gladden your every day's living.

XV

THE MASTER SENTIMENT FOR TRUTH

UNDERLYING every one of our actions is a desire. Though we are often unaware of its existence, a desire nevertheless is there, and when we perceive it, we call it a wish. If we undertake some activity in a good spirit, it is because our wishes are in accord with it. If, on the other hand, we approach a duty in a mean spirit, our state of mind is: "I shall do this thing because I feel compelled to, not because I wish to," and the probability is it will be done poorly. Our spirit is thus really our wish. It is more important to our body health than you can imagine, to do things in the right spirit, that is, to wish to do the things which each hour of the day it is right we should do.

Underneath our spirit or wish to do or not to do a thing, and giving rise to that wish, is a belief or sentiment. The only reason we do not wish to do a thing is that our sentiment is unfavourable, or that an opposing sentiment interferes with, or vetos the activity of the first. For example, the boy who shrinks from soap and water has a sentiment unfavourable to being washed. Develop his belief in the advantage of cleanliness, and his spirit or wish in the matter will become quite changed.

Once he has a large enough sentiment in favour of cleanliness, he will wish to be clean, and instead of any compulsion in the matter, he may be left to himself to apply his belief.

There are two factors which enter into the development of the boy's sentiment or belief—education and experience. Either factor in itself might produce a belief of a kind. For example, education as to the advantages of soap and water might bring him to the place where he could deliver a lecture on the subject, and profess to a profound belief in all that he said, and this without having so much as experienced the feel of soap. In such a case his belief would be abstract and intellectual.

On the other hand, without having been told anything about the advantages of cleanliness, he might have been compelled to use soap and water, and have developed a sentiment favourable to cleanliness through the benefits derived from experience. His belief then would be concrete and practical, but would lack intellectual support. To give the belief its full power, obviously the mind must perceive and body experience the advantages.

With the building up of the boy's intellectual belief in cleanliness, and as a material counterpart to it, there develops a system of energy paths through synapses or nerve centres of association cells in the brain. This intellectual system is located in those higher nerve levels which, as we have seen, are of late evolution, and are therefore less fixed than systems in lower levels. With repeated body action, on the other hand, the system of energy paths which is the correlative of conduct, becomes organized in the lower and more stable nerve levels. In the organization of the belief, this system is the more important of the two. If, however, through *mental training coupled with action,* a wedlock as it were, or integration between these material representatives of the intellectual and the animal is brought about, there develops a conviction, the automatic working of which will not be dependent on rewards or punishments.

All of us believe in truth, and, at least abstractly, regard a true line of conduct as preferable to a false. Like the boy in his belief respecting soap and water, we all have in our brains the material representative of the belief in truth which inspires a sentiment and a desire for truth; the majority of our activities are influenced, and possibly governed by it. There are, however, sentiments—many of those which have to do with pleasure and money—which render one more or less out of patience with, and opposed to the sentiment for what is rational. At least on special occasions, and sometimes six days in a week, these opposing sentiments would have us suppress and ignore the sentiment for truth.

The insurgent sentiments are successful in suppressing the sentiment for truth only because they have been reinforced with repeated action, whereas the sentiments favourable to eliminating harmful pleasures and selfish profits have only an educational or abstract basis. If the sentiment favourable to true conduct is to be made stronger, obviously it must be acted upon, and if the opposing sentiments are to be made weaker, they must be ignored. In this way, the sentiment for truth gradually will become the *master sentiment of the mind,* and, once this is brought about, there will be no trouble in exerting the will and compelling oneself to do one's duty. The most compelling wish flows fròm the strongest sentiment, and where the latter is for truth first, last, and all the time, every wish, like the magnetic needle of a compass, will point at all times in the one direction. As one of Dubois' patients put it: "The will drops passively into the beaten path which sentiment and reason (and we may add, *action*) have worn for it."

The more you are aware of truth in yourself, the greater is your self-respect; and the more you respect yourself, the stronger is your volition. So it is that we must set to work deliberately to develop through action this sentiment for truth. Every time you over-ride an unwise wish, and act in conformity with your sentiment for truth, you strengthen that sentiment. Conversely, every time your wish over-rides the sentiment, the latter is weakened.

Dr. McDougall puts this very clearly when he writes that some people "have not learned the awful power of habit, and have been content to say, 'This time I will not trouble to resist this desire, to suppress this impulse; I know that I can do so if I really exert my will.' Every time this happens, the power of volition is weakened relatively to that of the unorganized desires; every time the self-regarding sentiment masters an impulse of some other source, it is rendered, according to the law of habit, more competent to do so again—the will is strengthened as we say. And, when the habitual dominance of this master sentiment has been established, perhaps after many conflicts, it becomes capable of determining the issue of every conflict so certainly and easily that conflicts can hardly arise; it supplies a determining motive for every possible situation, namely, the desire that I the self shall do the right. So this motive, in the individual for whom it has repeatedly won the day in all conflicts of motives, acquires the irresistible strength of a fixed, consolidated habit; and, in accordance with the law of habit, as it becomes more and more fixed and invariable, it operates more and more automatically, *i. e.,* with diminishing intensity of its conscious aspect, with less intensity of the emotion and desire from which the habit was generated, and with less explicit reference to the persons in whose eyes the self seeks approval."

At first the strengthening of the sentiment will be uphill work; it will become easier day by day; finally you will wonder that you ever could have done differently. Whether, however, it be uphill work, or whether you often fall by the way, if unfalteringly you pick yourself up and continue to act on what is rational and true, it is inevitable that you will develop a passion for it. Once you have the real love of truth that comes through living it, in addition to thinking or believing it, the world that to-day is so weary and full of conflict will afford you such a wealth of satisfaction that you will wonder whence all the happiness comes.

Let us then get down to business. You need help. Very soon you will have the strength to travel entirely on your own resources, but for the present you will find assistance with your particular problems of great advantage. At times we all feel the need of "a guide, philosopher, and friend." If in your vicinity there be a medical man who has the time to devote to your special needs—not the kind of doctor who scribbles a prescription, and lets it go at that, but one who is interested in psychotherapy—you cannot do better than go to him, not for treatment of your symptoms, but for their eradication through strengthening of your volition and control.

Failing a physician, choose a friend whose opinion you value. A member of your own family is liable to be unsatisfactory, because his judgment in matters so closely related to his own interests, is liable to be biased. In making your choice, give preference to some one who believes that faith most truly reveals itself in action, and that, in prayer, backbone and effort speak louder than words Choose some one who has had his bumps, and who has come up, not gone down under them. Form your judgment of him on how he acted in some crisis in his own life. It is at such times the real man shows himself.

Go to your friend, and tell him that the teaching in this book appeals to you as common sense, and you wish him to help you to follow it. You do not wish him to give you sympathy or in any way to consider your feelings in the opinions he expresses. All you want is the unbiased truth as he sees it on matters of ordinary every-day living. Having received the truth from him, it is your responsibility to act on it, whether or not it jibes with your wishes. One thing he should positively refuse to listen to, is any remark about your body-symptoms.

Your body-symptoms are the result of energy paths in your brain which represent false beliefs. Until those paths die a natural death from impoverishment, through lack of culture, you are liable to experience symptoms. If you have symptoms, all right, be willing to have them. They are not going to do any harm. To talk about them helps to develop a belief in them. The symptoms are real, but the beliefs from which they spring are false, and to *ignore what is false is as important as to act on what is true.* At present you find it very difficult to control your thoughts, but you can control your tongue. You can refuse to say a word about your aches and pains to anybody but the doctor.

On the other hand, your belief that it is right not merely to believe in what is wise, but to act in conformity with it, needs all the culture you can give it. Think about the idea, talk about it, write about it, act about it, and infect everybody around you with your own enthusiasm in it. The attention you used to bestow on your tiredness, depression, and other symptoms, give henceforth to the deliberate defiance of them, by acting in a way utterly inconsistent with their existence.

Do not wait until next Wednesday or next Sunday to start following this course. Undertake it here and now. Take the family into your confidence without delay, and tell them that you realize you need their help. You may make mistakes: that is to be expected, but they must be made to realize that you are in earnest, and are making a great effort. It is *the making of the effort* which counts. If the family has any advice to offer, at least you will take the matter up with your friend, and will do your best to apply whatever of truth the advice contains. What you need from your relatives rather than advice, however, is encouragement. They soon will find out that a word of commendation where you have scored in putting into effect what is rational over a desire to the contrary, is worth reams of denunciation.

Tell all your friends that inquiry about your health is quite superfluous, that the whole subject of incapacity is taboo. Try to eliminate from your associates those mental paupers who are dependent on trouble as a topic of conversation; develop the friendship of people who are so busy in being of service to others that they have not the time to be selfish.

If your friends wish to help you, an occasional remark on their part about the ways in which you are helpful to other people, will afford a bigger boost than in telling you you are looking "just fine," or "so well," or "as though you had never been ill." You are going to struggle away from this atmosphere of body-inspection, and lay the whole emphasis on body-efficiency. Even if it be only a matter of washing dishes, it is the truth, the efficiency of the accomplishment that brings the thrills of joy. For you to realize, and have other people observe, that you can wash dishes, or do anything else, a little more efficiently than the next person, is a source of happiness and encouragement greater than to know, or be informed, that you are "*looking* just fine," while *feeling* decrepit.

Having in this way burned your bridges, let the next work be the development of stamina. Stamina is the stuff which makes us stick to it when we don't want to. It is stamina which enables us to sorrow and suffer in silence, and it is stamina which makes it natural for us to consider another's needs before our own. Stamina is the thing which constitutes courage and heroism, and the thing which above all others we admire in others, and which brings contentment in ourselves. It is the essence of personal power.

When stamina has dropped to a low ebb, everything looks hard, and is hard. Even walking a few blocks, or giving up some little pleasure, assumes the character of a hardship, and trivial indisposition occasions reaction utterly disproportionate to what is normal. When such a degree is reached the unwholesome state of affairs arises in which there has to be some sort of sugar-coated bait to entice a person to make an effort or a sacrifice which normally is the source of joy in living. It is the people who have been over-protected, those who have not had to use their volition, who have not had to forego their wants, and who have not suffered real privation, who are undeveloped in this respect.

The acquirement of stamina is obviously incompatible with doing what is easy. Conversely, the more we overcome and renounce, within rational limits, the more quickly do we develop stamina, and the less difficult do things appear. Stamina is acquired in two directions—positive and negative. One man will find it hard to walk four miles, but easy to lie down on the bed, and rest quietly for an hour in the afternoon. Another man would rather walk for two hours than lie down for one. The first man will gain stamina the more readily in a positive way by walking, and the second will gain it negatively by lying down, or giving in.

The more we funk in making reasonable effort, and the more we refuse to give up when giving up is wise, the poorer becomes the stamina with which to make effort or renunciation, and consequently the more burdensome every objectionable duty appears. On the other hand, stamina has a cumulative propensity, and gathers force with each act that over-rides resistance. Just as there is a habit with regard to some particular kind of work, so there is a habit of overcoming, whether it be overcoming a material obstacle or foregoing an unwise wish. Just as any particular kind of work by repetition is rendered almost auto-operative, so overcoming gets to the place where it is an unconscious art.

While considerable stamina can be accumulated by just blindly bucking into the line of greatest resistance, you will speedily obtain the results which encourage, by making your effort primarily along a line where it will count most effectually. While the time will come when at every opportunity you will do the difficult commonsense thing in preference to the easy, just for the sake of acquiring stamina and the happiness it affords, at present it is important that, while doing your best in a general way, you should get on top of one definite thing at a time, and stay with it until you master it.

Let us then first consider that which bears most directly on your indisposition. You have consulted a doctor; in fact, you have consulted more than one. They all have advised certain hours of rest, so much exercise, a regular time for meals, the taking of medicine, and so on. You have taken the medicine religiously, but what about the remainder of the prescription? Is it not a fact that you have carried out the part of the doctor's orders which has fitted in with your own wishes, and have forgotten that part which conflicted with unexpected happenings? Of course you have considered the latter more important than the treatment, but that was only because it was more in keeping with your wishes.

You have considered the unheeded part of the doctor's advice relatively unimportant. When you consult a doctor, do you go with the supposition that you can discriminate between what part of his advice is wise and what part is unessential, or is it to be conceded that it is purely your wishes which interfere with the carrying out of *all* the doctor prescribes? Let us suppose that you doubt his wisdom. It is quite legitimate to have such doubts, but the fact that you consulted a doctor at all is evidence conclusive that you are badly in need of the truth with regard to the course you should follow. Health is too important for you to remain content with an abortive opinion, and if you are not satisfied with one opinion, by all means have a consultation, and secure as many other opinions as are necessary to convince you regarding the true course.

Make sure of one point, however, and that is that you are looking for *truth* and not for some man who will toady to your wishes, and advise you in accordance with what you would like. Many a sufferer with " nerves " is unconsciously doing this very thing, wandering from doctor to doctor, carrying out the part of his advice which appeals to the imagination, forgetting what is distasteful, and, of course, as a consequence, finding no relief.

Here we have a practical example, embodying the type of thing which stands between you and health, between you and personal power. Your reason tells you that what the doctor advises is the true course to follow. Your feelings cry out against it, and induce you to use all sorts of sophistry to prove that *all* that the doctor has advised is not necessary, especially that part which relates to exercise. You do not understand how his advice can work out to your advantage; yet it is the truth, and your faith in truth to work out to your advantage only requires to be acted upon to be proved. You wish to make a compromise and escape a part of the advice which involves volition, the part upon which your cure depends. You have been saying, " Oh, how can I acquire self-control! " yet in this matter you are ready to give free rein to your wish to follow your own lethargic pursuits.

Is it any wonder you suffer from "nerves" when you insistently work against your own best interests? Do you not see that the cause of your trouble lies not at all in your body, but in a moral self which gives in to feeling, and is indifferent to making the body act on truth?

You can easily divide the doctor's advice into two parts, the part you are willing to carry out, and the part you do not wish to follow. Strange as it may seem, the first part is relatively unimportant, while the second part is essential to progress. Why? Because the carrying into effect of the second part will develop the stamina which is necessary for your perfect health.

Every time you put across the impulse which is resisted by an unwise wish, you score one. Henceforth, your moral self is just that much stronger. It requires only a small score to get rid of symptoms. Each point makes the next easier of attainment, and, before you realize it, the habit is yours. As you go on piling up the score, personal power increases; you rise in the world's estimation; more important, you rise in your own estimation, and living becomes really worth while.

Let your friend keep the score, and go to it with a release of the energy which has been yours all the time, but has been suppressed by a wrong idea of your own best interests. Nobody is going to compel you, but, with the knowledge that victory is now certainly within your reach, you will apply yourself deliberately to the most difficult part of your treatment. You will do it not only because it is breaking the shackles which fetter you, developing the stamina which will put an end to suffering, manufacturing the power that increases self-respect; you will do it because, more than all else, it is building the master sentiment for truth.

XVI

THE CONTROL OF EVERY-DAY ACTIVITIES

IN many respects the human body may be likened to a banking institution, the golden currency of which is energy. Unless we be the unfortunate heirs to some hereditary disease, we all come into the world endowed with a large reserve account. Each day of our lives we have a considerable income at our disposal, and many demands to meet. It is well we should consider our daily account, and make sure that our income is equal to our expenditure. No human body is insured against bankruptcy, and when our reserves are exhausted, business is no longer possible and the institution becomes but a memory.

Our daily income consists of food and sleep. When these are so regulated that they can be discounted into energy at par, they are adequate to meet a rational day's expenditure in work and play. Sometimes there arise emergencies when the output is necessarily excessive, and the reserve in consequence is considerably depleted. On other occasions, good opportunities present themselves for building up the reserve. Just as all banking institutions must follow true principles in the management of their resources, and carefully watch the fluctuations of the money market, so we should thoughtfully regulate our food, sleep, work, and play, and place them on an intelligent and business like basis of management.

There are two classes of people who neglect true principles in energy banking; the people of the one class are endowed with ox-like constitutions which *appear* to stand all kinds of abuse for years at a time. Such individuals carry a large reserve. At about the age of fifty, however, they usually go to the wall with one or other of the more serious organic diseases. The other class is composed of more sensitive persons who have considerable reserve, but who, through poor business methods, have so tied it up that they cannot draw on it in an emergency. They appear to be bordering continually on bankruptcy. Every time the balance of energy is overdrawn, there is a functional upset. The thing to note particularly is that both groups of individuals lose out as a result of following the course they wish, instead of the true course. It is only in the big outlook one can realize how it is that "freedom is obedience to law," and what poor policy it is to follow selfish interests.

When a financial concern shows signs of weakness, it is not sufficient that its manager should be visited by an expert financier, and simply be instructed in principles of financing; it is necessary that the books be opened, and a searching examination made of income, output, and reserve. Moreover, a general hazy idea of the use being made of the money is quite inadequate. There must be an accounting to the last cent.

To compare human energy to gold currency is an inadequate simile. Such energy represents not only material gold, but those spiritual attributes of existence which gold can never buy. If in our financial institutions we insist with such rigidity on daily accounting, on monthly returns, and periodical auditing, is it to be regarded as of too much trouble, once in a lifetime, to make a business-like examination of how we are using the priceless currency of our very lives?

The moment we begin to apply principles governing income and expenditure to any one individual, we are met by the assertion that such principles would undoubtedly be of advantage, only they interfere with something else, or something else interferes with them. It soon becomes apparent that no progress can be made, nor can the leak in the exchequer be discovered, until we have before us in black and white the total income and expenditure of the day.

The aim of every person who wishes to overcome "nerves," or to develop personal power, must be to *act,* and not to react. Just how accomplished you are in acting with reference to every-day events, may be demonstrated by the question: What are you going to do to-morrow, on Sunday, and on

Wednesday? You answer, "Well, that depends." Exactly, depends not on your self, but on other people, conditions, and things—depends on what happens to make you react, not on an intelligent policy of energy management. Have you so much energy that you can afford to expend it on everything which obtrudes itself upon your attention? Have you such a reserve that you can afford to do whatever tickles your fancy? These are some of the considerations in which you must become vitally concerned.

You have been wishing for some concrete way in which to apply truth to your living—some definite thing which you can *do* to acquire volition and control, something that will develop stamina along a line that really will count in every-day living, something which will add materially to your personal power. All right, here we have it. Get a large sheet of paper, and rule out a chart like the one on the next page.

In the column for the day write a list of everything you have done since rising in the morning. Let us say you got up at seven, washed and dressed in three-quarters of an hour. If getting up, washing, and dressing comprise a sequence of conduct which invariably is uninterrupted by some other activity, it is to be bracketed on the chart as a unit of time space from seven to seven forty-five. To designate it simply with letters or a sign, will suffice. If, however, between these activities this sec-

SELF-CONTROL DEVELOPMENT CHART

Name.................. Date..................

6 A. M.	Mon.	Tues.	Wed.	Thurs.	Fri.	Sat.	Sun.
7							
8							
9							
10							
11							
12							
1 P. M.							
2							

Continued to 12 P. M. Scale ½

tion of the day occasionally be made attractive by the morning mail, by a cigarette and a novel, or by a game of solitaire, only the part which invariably is an uninterrupted sequence of action, is to be bracketed as a unit.

The next item of the day—breakfast, takes to itself a bracket of twenty minutes or a half-hour, or, if you yourself have prepared the breakfast, that activity should also be given its correct time space on the chart. After breakfast, the letters ev. will indicate bowel evacuation. It is very important that this unloading of body toxins should occupy a fixed place in every day's program. The time position it occupies is not of as great importance as that it should occupy the *same* relative position *every* day.

If your life involves going regularly to business, your problem of living is greatly simplified, because the day then presents a comparatively small portion of instability and irregularity in energy expenditure. It is important, of course, that your hours of business should be analyzed carefully, especially if it appears that it is during that time you are over-drawing your account. Such is the love of the human being for pleasure and play, however, that the chances are a hundred to one that it is play, not work, which is eating into the reserve.

For obvious reasons, in a book like this, it is impossible to go into an analysis of all kinds of occupations in order to show in each of them, where nervous energy is unnecessarily expended. If, however, we consider you to be engaged in the care of the home—the most universal of all work—we can readily discover what it is about its management which involves unnecessary taxation of energy. What applies to housekeeping, in this regard applies equally to every other occupation, whether it be practising medicine or climbing the social ladder.

Of all occupations, housekeeping, or the management of the home, presents perhaps the largest quota of nervous patients. This is because, not being regarded in the light of a serious business, it offers a maximum opportunity for reaction to suggestion. While diversity of interests is essential to development of personality, it may be laid down as a rule that the more a person is freed from routine beyond what is rational in daily living, the greater the tax on the energies through haphazard reaction, and the more likely we are to find nervous symptoms.

Proceed with the recording of activities, including the items of both work and play, and indicate with a bracket the amount of time absorbed by each. After you have carried this out three or four days, each day recording literally every activity from rising to retiring, an inspection of the record will reveal many interesting and hitherto uncomprehended facts about your life.

It will be observed that your living divides itself

into five distinct groups of action. First, there are those activities which occur every day, such as rising, retiring, breakfast, lunch, dinner, and the like. This is about as far as some people go in what may be called the stable or *fixed daily* activities. Second, there is the *fixed periodical* group. These are the things which should be attended to once every few days, every week, or every fortnight. Third, a floating *incidental* group, under which come all irregular activities, outside of actual *emergencies,* which comprise the fourth group. Fifth, those activities which comprise *recreation and play,* and which should lie outside of business, but which nevertheless are an important part of living.

It will be noticed that the five groups occupy not only a variable position from day to day, but are mixed together on the same day much as impulse, rather than common sense, dictated. Among the fixed activities, you put in your orders for groceries at nine on one morning, the next day you just caught the afternoon delivery. One morning, after breakfast, you spread up the beds; after breakfast the next morning, you did the dusting, and so on.

All these activities are *bona fide,* but if the fixed items of your list have to be carried out each day *sometime,* why not have the peace of mind and conservation of energy incidental to a habitual time for attending to them? To carry them out by regular habit will require much less energy, and will prevent the waste of strength occasioned by incessant sub-conscious fear of omitting something which should be attended to.

With regard to the fixed periodical activities, notice how often they are put off on account of some insignificant attraction which obtrudes itself on the attention. Every doctor who has treated nervousness will tell the same story of patients who repeatedly have come to grief in the way the chart illustrates. Through giving in to impulse and desire, these patients have followed attractive pursuits for as many days a week as possible, and then felt compelled to cover all the fixed periodical activities in one day. Why should one be led around by the nose from day to day, instead of having an intelligently figured out program? Why let your business run you instead of you running your business?

Again, with the incidental group—there was a crate of raspberries which offered itself at such a low figure that the impelling impulse to buy it quite prevented consideration of the fact that Mrs. Vanity Fair was coming to dinner, and that the fruit jars had not been unpacked since the moving. The berries were bought, however, and could not be allowed to rot, so why discuss it? Naturally, however, the atmosphere would be nervous.

It is quite probable you have classified on your chart as emergencies many of the happenings which have caused you impulsively to drop some regular duty. It is well, therefore, that your emergency list should be analyzed carefully to make sure that it does not include items of the third or incidental group. The difference between the incidental group and emergencies is that the former may be attended to at a regular time, and not prove upsetting to system, whereas emergencies, of course, demand immediate attention.

The fifth group, recreation or play, too often spells death to duty. It is not only of advantage, but it is necessary, to have recreation, and enough of it, *at the right time;* too much play, however, or play mixed in with work, deprives one of the satisfaction that each is able to afford. In the case of the housekeeper, the part of the day's program which constitutes the business or work portion, too often is regarded as drudgery simply because it is neither play nor work, but a sort of hybrid that gives no satisfaction. Imagine any competent business concern, the manager of which whenever he felt like it, slipped out to gossip with a neighbour, or to attend a musicale, and so on. These things, of course, have their place; it is the making of the day a potpourri so that there is constant confusion, that dissipates energy, and in time tends to unbalance any one.

If business be habitual compromise between work and play, it is conducted under continuous conflict —under resistance to work, and sentiments opposed to play during working hours. You are thus the victim of two resistances; and the silent expenditure of emotional energy is a drain on your resources, greater far than would be the expenditure of energy on genuine hard work. Under these circumstances, little of real value is accomplished either through work or recreation. You are tired, not because you have worked, but because your moral self has tried to control two rebellious desires at one time, and has felt the strain.

To a fair degree, your tendency to nervousness can be gauged by the disorderliness of the five groups of daily activities on your chart. The chart will show the extent to which your wishes or impulses interfere with the systematic carrying out of duty and recreation. This habit of reacting, of going off at half-cock, whether it be to an unjust criticism or to an opportunity for play during business hours, discolours not partly, but entirely the fabric of living. To gain self-control under trying and turbulent conditions, you must first learn how to command the comparatively small impulse in ordinary every-day affairs.

There is no desire to dictate to you as to how much you shall work or as to how much you shall play. What do you think about it yourself? It is imperative that you get away from the policy of drift and reaction and live with your eyes open. It is essential that your moral self take a more active part in your living. Even if you cannot bring yourself to declare for more than one or two hours of actual work, once having determined what portion of the day is to be given to service, make that portion sacred to the truest thing about you, and secure the satisfaction it is sure to afford.

If you are not happy in your work, is it not because the spirit of earnestness and careful attention is lacking? No matter what your work, if you do it truly—if you have repeated it sufficiently often to be expert at it, you will find pleasure in doing it. It is only when the habit stage is reached that work will cease to make unnecessary demands on your energy.

The automatic condition cannot be brought about by doing your duties at one time on one day, at another time on the next, under leisurely circumstances on one occasion, and in a wild rush on another. Furthermore, even if others be working for you, should your knowledge of the work be only intellectual and abstract, you will live in constant fear of suffering humiliation through realizing that your employees *know* more about the work than you do. The first essential to freedom from depressing emotion, to peace of mind, and conservation of energy in any business, is expert knowledge *based on experience.*

So much for analysis of daily activities. Now the need quite obviously is to construct a tentative program, sufficiently comprehensive to include a regular place for each item of the fixed periodical duties. Have your chosen friend assist you in determining what will permit the most smoothly-running system. The more alike you can make the business parts of every day, and the more you can attend to fixed activities at the same time each day, the greater will be your saving of energy. It is not intended that you should wait for a set time to carry out a duty, except in the matter of meals, rising, and retiring. Outside of these fixtures, the great advantage lies in a *regular sequence* of duties and recreation, day in and day out.

You protest that you cannot become a machine. No, you cannot, but the fact is that until you become much *more* of a machine, you will continue so to waste your energy and muddle the days that you will rob yourself of the joy in living. Once the business part of your day becomes really stable and machine-like, you will find that your total effort for the same accomplishment is greatly reduced, your efficiency in what you accomplish markedly improved, and your self-respect very greatly enhanced.

Outside of real emergencies, the relative importance of each of the groups of daily activities is in accordance with the order of that group as outlined. The daily fixed activities are so important in relation to health and happiness that we shall consider them more fully a little later. When once this group is given a stable position on the day's program, we have pegs on which to hang the fixed periodical activities. No longer do we " take a notion " to clean up the week's work on one day, and as a result " bust the bank " for several days to follow, but we have a clear understanding with ourselves into just which place in the daily program each periodical activity fits, and furthermore, we have the duties of the week so distributed that they do not exact an exorbitant toll on any one day.

The program you draw up, is, of course, purely tentative. With experience you will find it rational to change things about until you discover the most smoothly running regime. As long as you change the program for definite reasons looking to efficiency, all well and good; the thing to try to avoid is allowing things to become " queered " just for the sake of some little selfish feeling or wish. You will avoid disappointment by having a regular time allotted for the reading of mail, for the order list and the putting in of orders, for the preparation of menus for the next twenty-four hours, and for the work of definitely planning the following day's activities. The more you can anticipate, the fewer will be the emergencies.

The group of fixed activities fall into three sections, each of which clusters about one of the regular meals. Between clearing-up after breakfast and preparing for lunch there occurs a time space which might well absorb one-sixth of the fixed periodical group. In the same period, there might possibly be opportunity for attending to one or more items on the incidental list as well. In any event the incidental list, if necessary, could receive attention in the afternoon interval.

It is when you seek to give earnest attention to your daily activities that incidental obligations will seem to crowd in upon you, and emergencies occur more than ever.

> "The best laid schemes o' mice and men
> Gang aft a-gley;
> And leave us naught but grief and pain
> For promised joy."

You will find, however, that what to-day you regard as an emergency, what to-day will upset your equilibrium, will in another month bow to your increased personal power, and be permitted to wait quietly to receive attention in its proper place.

One of life's constant problems is the discrimination between the transient incidental activities and emergencies. Willie comes in with a button off his pants. Is it an emergency? That should depend on the relative importance of the actual, not the suggested predicament, to the activity which is threatened with interruption. In too many instances, even although Willie has another pair of pants which he could slip on quite easily, impulsiveness, or the tendency to react without thinking, makes of the occurrence an emergency, when it should be simply an incidental item to be attended to at its regular time.

The great object in striving to live in conformity with a common sense program of daily activities is the power that such effort affords to overcome the innate tendency to impulsiveness or to act on emotion instead of reason. Let us recall Dr. McDougall's statement: "The first step toward moral conduct is the control of the immediate impulse." It may be a new idea that the disciplining of such a trivial impulse, as, for instance, that to sew on a button at the wrong time, is developing moral conduct; nevertheless, such procedure forms the very basis of moral stamina. Put through this A B C of self-control, and you will soon learn to rise above irrational irritability, anger, or fear.

Every earnest housekeeper should have attached to her clothing a pencil and note book. There is little use in keeping these on a table downstairs, or on a shelf upstairs; the note book is for use, not ornament. Whenever an item of the transient incidental group seeks to obtrude itself on regular business, let it be noted for consideration at the proper time. For example, there is the smudge on the front window, the message to Mrs. Vanity Fair about the committee meeting, the button to sew on Willie's pants, the reply to the letter from Jim's brother's wife, and so on. Each of these, if permitted, would be an emergency. By using a little self-control, each will cease to dominate your personality.

When the regular time arrives for attending to the incidental group, which gradually grows larger in your notebook, those things of greatest urgency and importance should, of course, be given first attention. If, however, there be several items of equal importance, choose to do first the one which you regard as the most difficult. The fact that you have accomplished the duty which taxes you most, will give you a surprising boost when you come to the other items on the list. On the other hand, if you put it off, the knowledge that there remains something which is unusually onerous will tend to suppress the enthusiasm and spontaneity which otherwise would lend zest to your undertakings.

Try to make the part or parts of the day you have determined to give to recreation, just as free from any thought of work as your business hours should be undisturbed by frivolity. Although it is quite legitimate to follow the line of least resistance in recreation, some planning will add greatly to its enjoyment. After all, there is but little pleasure in idleness, and direction of attention is essential to full satisfaction in play as in work.

While the formulation of a program is essential, the real work, of course, consists in applying what you have planned. You will find that the greatest difficulty lies in the frequency with which you are disposed to consider incidental items as more important than regular fixed activities. Unless you check yourself in this, you will upset the latter with the former. The greater importance of incidental activities is not a fact; it is a state of mind, due to the attractiveness of what is novel, and the wish to procrastinate what you regard as drudgery.

Drudgery always will be drudgery unless it be rendered more auto-operative through machine-like routine, scientific efficiency, and improvement of the spirit in which it is undertaken.

It is the habit of putting off the unpleasant, of leaving trivial tiresome duties partly unfulfilled, which makes for exasperation and wastes much good energy. How often, for example, the postponed task of returning articles to their proper places, occasions a prolonged and wearying search when next they are required; how often because of the bother involved in having to return to secure a warmer wrap or rubbers, the body is made to run an irrational risk; or again, how frequently a decayed tooth is allowed to poison the system before the unpleasantness of having it treated is endured!

Another tendency which will threaten the auspicious carrying out of your program, is that of failing to put aside some interesting activity, when the regular time arrives to begin a duty of one of the higher groups. This we shall consider more definitely in the following chapter.

You now commence the daily systematic development of self-control. This evening you consult your program and notebook, and enter your list of activities for to-morrow in the proper column of the Volition and Control Development Chart. To-morrow evening, before repeating the process for the day following, you check up the discrepancies between what you planned, and what you accomplished for the day. The discrepancies will be due to real emergencies, transient incidents, or planning more than you could accomplish. In the beginning do not plan extravagantly; it is likely to prove discouraging. It would be irrational not to allow your program to be upset by real emergencies. It would show lack of nervous stamina to have it upset by impulsiveness or by transient incidents of no greater significance than " I want."

Let your friend be the judge of what constitutes a legitimate emergency. If he regards as only incidental what you have classed as an emergency, he should be able to show clearly how in future such an occurrence can be reduced to its proper classification. Let him give 100 per cent. for a day which is lived as you planned, and deduct 5 per cent. for each lapse in control of the situation. You will then be able to watch your self-control grow, and see your moral self rise step by step in personal power, until you look beyond the confines of the " I wants " and " I don't wants," and taste the joy that volition and control inevitably bring.

It will be seen at once that this scheme grapples with the weakest thing in us, namely, the tendency to follow the line of least resistance instead of what is rational and true. It will be realized also that by following the plan here outlined, on the one hand, volition is trained to put through the right thing at the right time, and, on the other, control is developed to give up desires which, indulged at a wrong time, are untrue and unprofitable, even though they might afford an immediate and transient pleasure. Here then is the ideal means of making the sentiment for truth the master sentiment of the mind. Lay the emphasis on action. This is needed to strengthen what, in the past, has been a more or less sentimental belief.

The plan is not as difficult as it appears. If you will give to it half the attention you would give to learning to play the piano, or some other accomplishment which could not begin to compare with it in importance, it will render most encouraging results. If for one month you will devote to the analysis of your daily activities but fifteen minutes of earnest attention each evening, it will bring you a surprising degree of relief and satisfaction. Of one thing you may feel sure, the more difficulty you experience in carrying out the plan, the more badly you are in need of it. In the beginning of its study, no art is unconscious. While unconscious (or automatic) good habits form undoubtedly the ideal at which to aim, these cannot be acquired without considerable analysis and conscious attention to detail.

There is no short cut to the radical cure of "nerves;" there is no panacea for preventing waste of energy. We have to arrange our living in such a way as to render our income and output fair and rational. To wail about tiredness and overwrought nerves is only an indictment of our energy management. If we have neglected it in the past, that is all the more reason for getting down to business at present.

The thing we admire most in other people is efficiency and common-sense, and, if we are to regard ourselves with anything approaching satisfaction, it must be through a realization that, at least, we are doing our duty.

> "The longer on this earth we live
> And weigh the various qualities of men
> The more we feel the high, stern-featured beauty
> Of plain devotedness to duty,
> Steadfast and still, nor paid with mortal praise,
> But finding amplest recompense
> For life's ungarlanded expense
> In work done squarely and unwasted days."

XVII

SELF-CONTROL IN ORDINARY LIVING

EVERYBODY'S day is made up of four fundamental occurrences—eating, exercise, rest, and work. Upon the reasonable regularity of these depend health, happiness, and general prosperity. The most of human suffering and misery is occasioned through habitual irregularity in these daily experiences.

Since no man can live to himself alone, all men are to some extent dependent for regular living upon the co-operation of others. One may try very hard to regulate the business of living, and under any circumstances may accomplish much by way of conserving nervous energy. Unless, however, there be a fair degree of co-operation, particularly in the home, a power of adaptation as exceptional as it should be unnecessary, is required. In considering the overcoming of weakness and the development of personal power in any one member of a family, each other member will do well to consider also his own weakness. The head of a household especially, should take stock of just how much matters may be improved through giving more heed to co-operation, and through seeking to overcome his own tendency to react to suggestion.

In the matter of meals, it is usually true that more irregularity is occasioned by lack of co-operation on the part of those for whom the meals are prepared, than on the part of those who make the preparation. Too often the housewife is virtually persuaded into a sacrifice of system and method, by a husband whose ox-like constitution does not render him so immediately sensitive to the baneful effects of disordered eating and living. Men are frequently disposed to consider business as of more importance than the principle of regularity. They fail to realize that personal power in business, as in other things, is proportional to ability to make first things come first.

Many a man will argue that his particular business demands that he be irregular. This, however, is only because he is in bondage to it. What habits do we find on the part of men in big business—the men of great executive ability? Have they made their way by neglecting regularity? By no means. The very secret of their success lies in the fact that they possess in business affairs an excellent self-command; sufficient, for example, on the stroke of the hour to cease dictating an important letter in order to keep an appointment. Can any business demand be more urgent than that of attention to illness and injury? What do we find among physicians and surgeons with the largest practices? For the most part machine-like regularity in the essentials of living, at least five or six days in the week.

Were it not so, how long would a surgeon keep his health and steadiness of nerve? Clear, keen thinking is impossible when the blood is impregnated with toxins, as is inevitable with habitual irregularity in eating.

After all is said, it is simply a matter of feeling, not of reason, which makes people habitually irregular. Ofter it is the feeling that work demands it; more often it is indulgence in pleasure. Always it is that one lacks self-control, that is, reacts too readily to suggestion.

Laudatory as are the efforts of industry, true industry does not necessitate disordered living for oneself or a disregard of the industry of others. The secret of productiveness is co-operation, in other words, a dovetailing of activities so that the good of all may not become subordinate to the irrationality of one. Matters of business, whether big or small, should be viewed as insignificant in comparison with duty to self and to the rights of others. The man who allows himself to be habitually dominated by business, classes himself as a thing of less importance and less power, and shows he has less regard for himself, than for that to which he takes second place.

It is only in a minority of instances that the passion for material gain or worldly prestige is responsible for eclipsing rationality and co-operation. It is comparatively seldom that, through work alone, a man defeats his own end by causing ill health and feeble capacity in "the last of life for which the first is made." In the vast majority of cases, as we have had occasion to observe, it is the inordinate love of pleasure which defies the attempt to live in accord with true principles; and this prevails with regard to eating more perhaps than in anything else.

There is no need to preclude the pleasures of life. In themselves they are of great advantage, but it is their relationship and their extent to which consideration has to be given. It would be a deprivation not to be entertained by one's friends, not to drink rich and delicious concoctions, not to eat fancy cakes, ices, and sweets, but it is well to consider just how often in the week it is in the interest of one's well-being so to indulge. It is most enjoyable and profitable to attend a banquet or sumptuous dinner, but just how frequently? Have you considered the consequences of habitual overindulgence in this respect?

There are two kinds of irregularity in eating; first, in the time at which food is taken, and, second, in the quality and quantity eaten. Where food is plain and wholesome, the quantity eaten may be made largely dependent on the interval between meals, but where it is fancy or rich in character, common-sense considerations are apt to be lost sight of. Where both kinds of irregularity in eating are habitual, is there need to look further for a cause of chronic indigestion, and for suffering of the point of view and of the body as a whole? Is further explanation needed for irritability, general impoverishment of vitality, emaciation, and a dyspeptic view of life generally, or of obesity, mental and muscular torpidity, with tiredness, headaches, and depression?

A volume might be filled with a description of suffering caused by irregular eating. It would, however, more likely cater to the love of what is morbid than strengthen the sentiment for truth. Until the end of time, there will be the blindness which sees only the disability and the bottle of medicine, and there will be the love of pleasure which will find a cause for suffering anywhere and everywhere but in one's own irregular way of living.

Where there is no organic disease, all suffering is the result of unwise living. Sometimes we pay the penalty of another's lack of wisdom; usually it is our own. There is no need to consider the effects of unwise living except to realize that its attractiveness is purely on the surface. The thing we should study, that to which we should give our whole attention, is what constitutes rational living. To bestow attention on morbid conditions will afford little wisdom as to what is rational.

When a man becomes a crank about what he eats, he gets hold of his trouble at the wrong end Such an one can give you all the properties of foods, and tell you what will be harmful to your liver, kidneys, and each of your other internals, and he can picture vividly what is happening to his food from the moment it enters his mouth. Were he to dissociate his point of view from the morbid, and be content to eat three plain meals daily, each at its regular time, five hours apart, without any extras between times, he would soon forget that he had a stomach. The more we switch our attention from morbid conditions to the art of living as nature intends us to live, the more analysis concerns itself with conduct and wise management, the more we shall realize that regular living leaves little opportunity for illness to occur or continue.

As a matter of fact, before the function of an organ becomes deranged through poor management, it is able to carry out work greatly in excess of what normally should be required. Most of us could continue to carry on with but a part of one lung, only one kidney, and, for that matter, without any stomach at all! The body has been well equipped for emergencies. It is only where through flagrant irregularity, people institute a continuous series of emergencies that one or more of their organs becomes unable to keep up the pace.

Often associated with irregularity of meals, and adding to its ill effects, is irregularity in outdoor muscular exercise. Normally, many of the poisonous by-products of assimilation are gotten rid of through muscular activity. Exercise when taken in fresh air, not only helps to eliminate the body toxins through the skin, the respiration, the kidneys, and the intestines, but it insures good work on the part of all the body organs through stimulation of the circulation and oxygenation of the blood. Rich foods may be adequately disposed of by prolonged, vigorous, muscular work, but habitually to under-exercise, and to over-eat, will sooner or later occasion suffering.

Torpidity of muscles and of mind usually go hand in hand. Some psychologists go so far as to say that we think with our muscles. Certainly muscular actions reveal more truly the intention, mind, and character of man, than do words or anything else about him. If the mind controls the muscles, it is equally true that the activities of the muscles determine the character of the energy paths in the brain. This being so, it is evident that our state of mind is to a great extent dependent on the training of our muscles.

Every normal person should walk at least four miles a day. Where it has not been a habit, it will be a little taxing at first, and should be extended by degrees. Everything to which we are not used, requires an effort. Possibly in no better way can the nervous patient who is flabby and sedentary develop stamina, and get rid of the constant sense of effort in all undertakings, that by toning up his muscles and general system through outdoor exercise.

While there is a recreative value in making exercise attractive as for example by a game of golf or tennis, when this is not feasible it is helpful to remember that we develop stamina more quickly by getting away from what is sugar coated, and by doing what is rational, if for nothing else than to give ourselves increased self-command. In daily exercise, as in other things, it may be convincingly demonstrated that what in the beginning may be regarded as an inveterate bore, has but to be persisted in to become not only tolerable, but a source of genuine pleasure.

The point of great importance in developing health and strength through muscular exercise, is, as in other things, the fixing of one definite time in the day for carrying it out, and the arranging, before starting, as to the distance to be covered and the direction to be taken. To try to make up for delinquencies on one day, by over-doing on another, is worse than foolish. It is the regular and graduated exercise, day in and day out, that not only brings the best development, but finally affords real exhiliration and pleasure.

Partly dependent though we may be on the cooperation of others in having our meals at regular hours, we are for the most part free lances in the matter of rising and retiring. Irregularity in rising is much more of a radical disturbance to the day than an irregular meal. " He who loses an hour in the morning is looking for it all the rest of the day." We can blame nobody but ourselves if we upset the effectiveness and satisfaction of the day by lying in bed after the regular hour for rising.

People generally do not realize that over-indulgence in sleep is quite as harmful as lack of muscular exercise. While the latter takes away from muscular virility and produces body flabbiness, over-indulgence in sleep saps stamina and creates moral flabbiness. The forcing of impulses through sleepy brain paths, like overcoming resistance in any other duty, calls for volition and stamina. Habitually to give way to one's feelings, when heavy with sleep, is to foster nervous weakness, whereas to act on pre-determined principles of rising, develops the general art of self-control. We should use not only the intellectual part of our minds to determine a rule with reference to rising, but also our moral part to compel obedience to what we have determined.

In this matter of getting up in the morning, there are many plausible excuses for giving way to our feelings, and they always appeal to us with much greater force just when the alarm goes off. The auto-suggestions that we are over-wrought, over-tired, not very well, too hard worked, and other irrational fancies which we should not think of applying to other normal human beings like ourselves, not only support our self-indulgence at such times, but echo in the subconscious mind when other disagreeable activities tempt us to funk. The half-waking state is an ideal time for such auto-suggestions to take hold. It is, therefore, taking grave chances when, in a condition so vulnerable to suggestion, we become too sympathetic with our irrational feelings.

The principle to be applied to rising from rest is that to be applied in all activities, namely, to determine in our most wide-awake rational moments, how we shall act, when the temptation to give in to our feelings assails us. It is not in saying prayers or in singing hallelujahs that moral stamina is acquired, but rather in acting on carefully determined principle, instead of on feeling, in such everyday commonplaces as getting up in the morning.

Should people hobnob, have a game of whist, or sit and read stories before breakfast, it would be regarded as somewhat of a joke, or as rank dissipation. On the other hand, to overstep by an hour or two the regular time for going to bed in order to enjoy these same diversions, and to make it up by sleep in the morning, fits in so felicitously with feeling that it is all too readily acquired as a habit.

Be it emphasized, there is no desire to preclude pleasure. When, however, the time of going to bed is habitually interfered with by pleasure, when there is so much pleasure that one is unable to get up at a reasonable hour, so much pleasure that breakfast is served at 10:30 instead of 7:30, so much pleasure that we cannot get rid of the toxins of one richly prepared meal before the next pleasure feast arrives, is it not time to consider whither body and soul are drifting?

The time is coming, if it be not already here, when the best type of physician will refuse to treat a case of chronic indisposition without being furnished with a time chart of each day's total activities. In many a case of chronic functional upset the patient is not looking for advice as to the cause of his disability, and would not think of imposing on himself discipline sufficient to prevent the occurrence of symptoms. What he wishes is not advice, but a bottle of medicine which will enable him to continue living in accord with unwise wishes.

Consider for a moment the folly of putting stimulating medicine in a stomach which rebels against meals at habitually irregular hours, or which staggers under six to ten course meals, served as often as three times a week! Think of the absurdity of prescribing tonics for people who are too sedentary to walk a mile! Consider the crime of giving bromides, veronal, aspirin, and what not, to people who are so irregular in going to bed and in getting up that nature rebels, and shows her disapproval by causing insomnia! Reflect on the nonsense in giving medicine, electricity, hydrotherapy, or anything other than honest education and persuasion, to correct an insatiable love of pleasure!

Should you perchance be suffering from fatigue, insomnia, irritability, depression, vague aches and pains, headache, and any of the other consequences of irregular living, you should cease placing your hope in the pill, the powder, and the potion, and get down to the business of balancing your day so as to avoid excesses. Do it earnestly, and within a month your symptoms will become but a memory.

From a spiritual or a moral standpoint, human society may be divided into two great classes—the co-operative, and the anti-social. The one merges into the other, but the extremes are easily recognized. The members of the co-operative group, through psychical or moral development, accept complacently the fact that they owe society a reasonable share in the toil which makes for progress. Through lack of experience or education, or in virtue of some special benefaction, individuals comprising the anti-social group have not grown away from the atmosphere of compulsion experienced in childhood. The anti-social person has a deep distaste for obedience to law, whether it be natural law or the law of man. In other words, he is resistant to what nature and man require of him, and of course he suffers, because nature at least is inexorable.

The co-operative individual regards work or service as the most important thing in life, and realizes that his capacity for service depends on his good health. Therefore he conforms to those principles which enable him to safeguard what he considers the thing of greatest importance. Into the calculations of the anti-social individual, however, work enters as something which has to be endured, rather than as the thing for which he must keep fit by the regularity and discipline of his habits. Such an individual has a twisted idea of what comprises satisfaction in life, and has made the mistake of regarding freedom from work and the quest of pleasure as the chief ends of man.

There is no desire to press the classification other than to have you realize that the co-operative person is the happy member of society, whereas the anti-social individual is the Ishmael, whose "hand will be against every man and every man's hand against him."

In the past, if you have been living on a basis of warring compromise, if you have had the feeling that you would render service only in so far as you were compelled to, and would follow your own unwise desires as far as you thought you could get away with them, realize now, once and for all, that such a policy will keep you in everlasting bondage to fear, dissatisfaction, and anger.

The wish underlying service, or the doing of anything that is helpful, is the factor which determines the effect such service will have on your self-respect. To work or serve under compulsion makes you regard yourself as a slave or an underling, whereas to serve because it is your duty, and because you owe it to the world, allows you to regard yourself in the light of a man who is entirely on the square with his fellow-men.

To neglect your duty to society, because you are relieved of the necessity of serving, sooner or later will bring the lack of self-respect which is manifested in discontent and mental suffering. You must face the fact frankly—you cannot gain or keep self-respect, unless you take an adequate part in the total toil of the world. You may have a fine æsthetic sense and love of what is beautiful, quite possibly you can exact homage from people less fortunate in worldly possessions, and you may have the false pride and power of a tyrant, but you will remain a stranger to the satisfaction which comes from true self-regard.

You probably will agree that to love is to serve, and that to serve is to love. Until we have served from choice, not from compulsion or in expectation of personal profit, we can never experience the love of serving. It is only after we exert ourselves to serve without thought of return or even of thanks, that we finally realize the love of service. The wishing and the doing are essential to each other's welfare. In the same way, if we would develop the sentiment for what is true, we will force ourselves to co-operate and to act in conformity with justice towards all men. Think of the professed love of truth on the part of people who will not give up a personal desire for truth's sake. Do they comprehend the meaning of the word? What a stranger to truth is he who finds only loss, self-denial, and sacrifice, in the privilege of service to others!

Without good health we serve to great disadvantage, and so are handicapped in earning happiness. What a big responsibility this places upon us in the matter of being ill! Is it possible that giving way to unwise wishes has had anything to do with our illness, or, what is more to the point, can it be possible that indulgence of our unwise wishes is interfering with our gaining perfect health and strength?

In reconstructing our future, the paramount consideration is to be given to fitness for service. Everything which interferes with the maintenance or regaining of health of body and mind, must be discarded. This means that those desires which interfere with rational regularity of meals, exercise, rising, and retiring, are to be regarded as unwise or selfish wishes which interfere with the true development of ourselves through service to others.

Henceforth, work and the opportunity to serve must be given a more exalted position in our conception of what comes first in life, and pleasure must be given a subordinate position. In the day's program, not only must we have something which is solid and true, but we must come to feel that the solid and true part is the most important feature of the day, and that all else is subsidiary.

Perhaps you have been wondering just what you can do in the way of regular work that will suit your particular disposition. You would like to have one section of your daily program represent something which will count for happiness, health, and an abiding peace of mind. As you look over the list, however, you fail to find anything attractive. You may go on looking forever, but you will never find anything really worth while which, in the beginning, you would *like* to do. At first *any* true work is hard. It is in the mastery of what is difficult that happiness lies. Why, therefore, seek what is easy? At first you will do it somewhat crudely; step by step the technique will become more perfect, and the art more unconscious; finally, the mastery which systematically worn nerve paths inevitably bring will afford that exhiliration in work which is the greatest joy in living.

To be sure, if, at sometime in the good old days, you were trained to some special kind of work, much of the pioneering in nerve path finding will have been accomplished. With time the energy paths through the synapses have become partly effaced, but well-regulated driving of impulses, repeated at the same hour each day, will soon clear the passage, and evolve a nervous mechanism that automatically is a source of benefit to the world and satisfaction to yourself.

If there be no potentialities of the past to convert into producers for the present and future, give the preference to some type of work of which the altruistic serviceableness is apparent. It should, however, be a line of work which requires development, and which will become the aim of a lifetime, and not the hobby of a week or a month. There is no need to be romantic in the choice—the application of scientific management to the home, the training of the child on psychological principles, some special line of nursing, teaching, or entertaining; gardening, poultry raising, all such will be found to be in keeping with what is true and what earns happiness. Whatever line of work you take up, conduct it a little more scientifically than anybody else.

Having once chosen your objective, fix definitely the hours of the day it is to absorb. Be sufficiently earnest to turn a deaf ear to all pleasure during those hours, and make them of first importance in your life. It is only in this way that you can develop the right spirit and perfect satisfaction in your undertaking.

If the hours you devote to work be too many, you are defeating your purpose; if too few, you are deprived of just so much opportunity to derive satisfaction and personal power from your efforts. The greatest happiness in life depends upon the care with which we discriminate as to amount. What becomes of discrimination when we are indifferent to fixing a limit either to work or to play, and are weakly dependent on commands or suggestion for the shaping of the day?

Should it be that you are overworked, and belong to the small band of beings who have to learn how to play; if, by chance, you have become a slave to a routine of living which is irrational in its neglect of recreation; the indication is, of course, to develop the stamina that will enable you to carry out what you realize to be the true course, and to defy the forces, or break down the barriers which hold you in bondage.

Perhaps, like many another, you have been telling yourself that if you wish to overwork, it is entirely your own concern, that if you wish to have a good time at the expense of your health, you are the one who suffers; in short, that it is nobody else's business how you run your own life. If only such reflections were true, how very much less suffering the world would hold!

The fact is, however, that you are a cell in the living social body. It is impossible for you to suffer, and to cease to carry out your function, without the social body as a whole, and particularly those cells in the special group to which you belong, suffering likewise. Get away from the idea that your part is unimportant to the family or to the world at large. If you be not important as a help, you are at least of concern as a hindrance, and you alone can correct that. The constitution of the social body is such that, until you are dead and buried, your every action affects the welfare of all men.

We may go over again and again the problems of existence, in the end they all come back to the one question: *why* are we living? If we be living for our own interests in contra-distinction to those of society as a whole, we shall always feel dissatisfied, and travel through life in discontent. On the other hand, if our ambition be to emulate others in promoting the happiness and welfare of the whole of which we form a part, we shall, in innumerable unexpected places, hear the benediction which echoes in the heart of every man who follows truth.

So important are established habits in determining self-control in ordinary living that this chapter will hardly be complete without some word on the dangers lurking in haphazard methods of training children and the corresponding advantages of rational procedure. As stated before, ordered nerve paths make an ordered mind, and ordered activities make both. It is through systematized activities that a child's mind becomes ordered. Happy-go-lucky methods make a happy-go-lucky mind. Attention to principle and discrimination as to what it involves, form the very foundation of mental health and happiness. It is highly important, therefore, that, as early as possible, a child should not only be taught principle, but should be thrown on his own resources to carry out what he has learned. This is impossible when he is allowed to play with the hose-nozzle, but not with the tap; with the old bottle, but not with the jardiniere, and so on.

Two of the negative faults of childhood which need special check are " fussing " and disobedience. Insolence and disrespect are the outgrowth of disobedience, and will never show themselves if authority is what it should be. By " fussing " is meant lack of self-control, as manifested in dissatisfaction with, and rebellion against, what is wise and necessary. Of all faults, from the standpoint of " nerves," " fussing " is perhaps the most threatening to the future health of a child. It is the selfish wish crying aloud for satisfaction, and in proportion to the success it meets, there is engendered the tendency of life-long capitulation to the " I want " over duty.

Disobedience, the other negative fault mentioned, is either intentional or unintentional. The former is easily recognized. The cause of unintentional disobedience is inattention, or forgetting. Attention is often an act of volition or effort, dependent on moral stamina. It is so much easier not to be bothered. On the establishment of the habit of attention, however, will depend in great measure the child's nervous stability.

Of the positive habits we should seek daily to have a child acquire, cleanliness, punctuality, orderliness, and industry are of outstanding importance. These four positive factors, if systematically developed during childhood, will go a long way toward insuring a life of nervous stability, usefulness, and happiness. None of these virtues become habits through a following of the line of least resistance.

In all our disciplining we should realize something of the unfairness to a child of allowing exceptions to occur in the building of a moral habit. Every time a child "gets away with it," twice as much persuasion is necessary to bring him back to the same moral level. It is in proportion to the chances of getting away with it that the wish to do what is wrong is sustained and that mental conflict is developed. If there is one habit more than another the formation of which we should seek to prevent, it is that of indecision. We should strive to bring the child to the place where the unwise wish is automatically dismissed with the reflection, "of course that is not to be thought of." Only appeals to the intelligence, well founded appreciation of good conduct, and *consistency* in discipline, will bring this about.

Nervous health depends on ability to adapt oneself to new and possibly shocking experiences, and the time and place for the acquirement of adaptation is not after a child has left its home to be buffeted about in a callous and unconcerned world, but while it has at hand the guiding mind of a sympathetic parent. During this time, when the mind and nervous system can be adapted to evil as never in later life, the opportunities of using a child's experiences to make teaching practical are unfortunately all too few.

Two forms of exposure of little children are prevalent—the one, exposure in the back-yard to sand, mud, bumps, scratches, and even cuts; the other, exposure to the vagaries of a nurse-maid. The former though cheap is valuable; the latter is both expensive and harmful. While some nurse-maids are more valuable associates for children than the parents, there are others whose influence is pernicious. The significant point is the uncertainty of the nurse-maid environment as compared with the definite advantage of the back-yard.

The nurse-maid usually has charge of a child in the most formative period of its life; she associates with it for the greater number of its waking hours; she protects it from trivial painful experiences, the advantages of which no amount of abstract teaching can supply; possibly she also exposes it to mental perversions which some day will give a most unfortunate twist to the child's mind. The exposure to the back-yard, which makes for independence and grit is true protection, while the so-called protection of a possibly malignant mental influence may prove to be damaging exposure. Whatever the condition, the teaching of independence of spirit cannot be commenced too early.

One of the greatest needs of the child is protection against the oft-repeated suggestion of ill health. The strongest innate tendency of childhood is imitation, and in the home where tiredness, headaches, and depression are prevalent, and where immediate attention is given to the imitated symptoms, the child is fortunate if it escapes being educated and persuaded into indisposition. A child brought up in such an environment, when pressed into any activity which requires painstaking effort or suffering volition, almost invariably cloaks its desire to funk with: " It makes me nervous," " I am too tired," or " My head aches." While this may be of little consequence on one or two occasions, none of us can react in the same way week after week without acquiring the habit; and if desire to funk be called tiredness, real fatigue very readily may be considered prostration.

Too careful attention cannot be given to the type of sympathy we employ, and to the things with which we associate it in the child's mind. There is an innate desire for sympathy in all of us, and more so in children, and it is easy for craving along this line to become so excessive that it makes children sympathy mendicants instead of men and women. Sympathy is the well-spring of love, and to withhold it where it would be helpful is a grave error. It is this matter of *helpfulness,* however, which must be given careful consideration.

A result of excessive and misplaced sympathy is to be seen in what is described by Freud as the Oedipus complex. This is an affection between father and daughter, or mother and son, so overbalanced that when the time arrives for the natural breaking away to take place, there is nothing in life which is sufficiently attractive to cut the ties of parental attachment. While on the face of it, this appears very beautiful, it is unnatural, unhealthy, and circumscribing in its effect.

If we could be so honestly, there are none of us who would not be wealthy. If used wisely, wealth can be one of life's greatest blessings; it is an unfortunate fact, however, that the over-protection it affords occasions more mental suffering than any other factor. What can we expect of children who are so protected that they are given private education to avoid associations which might be corrupting; who are driven to school in automobiles, not allowed to cross the street without a nurse in attendance, who have servants to see that they are properly dressed, to pick up their toys, to insure their being on time for meals, and to dance attendance to their wishes? Where, in such an environment, is a child to acquire independence of thought or action, decision and responsibility in every day living, stamina to endure what is unpleasant, volition to overcome obstacles, control to forego unwise wishes, or adaptation to the seamy and shocking side of life?

The over-protection of wealth seems to lead naturally to an exalted regard for pleasure. Those things which are unpleasant, even work, study, or duty, are too often allowed to be set aside for whatever gives promise of considerable pleasure. In the homes of the rich instances where little children give box parties at the theatre, issue engraved invitations to luncheons, rule with authority over servants, and the like, are growing in frequency. What, oh what! does the future hold for such as these? Ennui, dissatisfaction, disgust, and dejection—not only these, but a condition which is even more threatening to mental health.

Rational protection is afforded, finally, not through suppressing animal energy, or sympathizing with precociousness, but by encouraging a wide range of pleasant and unpleasant experiences, while at the same time watching the reaction and teaching adaptation. Careful investigation should be made to discover the cause of failure in adaptation to any kind of physical or spiritual experience. It is more likely to be found in the attitude of the parent than in disability on the part of the child.

It may be a little difficult for some readers to realize the direct bearing of all these considerations on "nerves." If, however, parents will undergo the self-denial, and take the pains necessary to carry out systematically the teaching of the latter part of this chapter and live regularly themselves, it is safe to say that not only will relations of mutual love and respect be fostered, but there will be established in the children that orderliness of energy paths which underlies every strong sentiment for truth, and which through life will prove the nucleus of rational independence, self-esteem, and personal power.

XVIII

THE CONTROL OF PARENTAL LOVE AND OF ANGER

IT will be realized that command over our activities in ordinary everyday affairs, while an important gain, is, nevertheless, only a first step in the acquirement of the general art of self-control. Such matters as regularity and system, as a rule touch us but lightly, that is, call forth a comparatively mild degree of emotion. In the more personal relationships, however, where such strongly emotional sentiments as love of children and hate are stimulated, we seem at times fairly driven to act irrationally and in a manner contrary to our best interests.

In our deep reverence for the beauty of mother-love, we are too often disposed to forget that the only thing which raises it above the love of the lioness for her whelps, or the maternal regard of the bear for her cubs, is the æsthetic and intellectual embellishment of the animal instinct. In the mother of the child, as in the mother of the cub, identically similar animal impulses impel her to rush to the protection of her offspring, to shelter them, to feed them, to play with them, and to die in their defence if necessary. The tender emotion is shared alike by Beauty and the Beast.

It has been pointed out that while human beings have inherited from the brute creation instincts and emotional impulses identical with those of the lower animals, civilization has advanced to such a degree of complexity that to employ these innate impulses without considerably modifying them with reason will lead to the defeat of the very desires which bring them into action.

Beautiful as is mother-love or sympathy, it is not an unmixed blessing. Like everything else, it has to be balanced by careful discrimination, for it may wreck the lives of those on whom it is bestowed inordinately. Moreover, it must listen to the dictates of principle, and often must crucify itself by deliberately inflicting suffering on the object of its affection. Human mother-love, as raised above that of ordinary animal tendency, finds its test in whether it will over-ride the innate desire to protect and to indulge—whether it will suffer, as inevitably it must suffer, for the sake of what, in the calm light of reason, is rational and true.

At the bottom of nearly all nervousness and much sickness, lies over-protection at a time in life when the body and the mind have the elasticity to acquire adequately the valuable art of adaptation. In families where there is an "only child," so frequently does it come to grief nervously in later life that all parents will do well to give careful consideration to the why and wherefore.

Much has been written, and much more conjectured, about the significance of temperament and inheritance. If such considerations form a part of a study of eugenics, and therefore be undertaken with a view to correction of defect, there is value in them. What is the use otherwise of giving attention to so-called hereditary defects about ourselves or our children? What is the value of considerations which all too readily afford an excuse for the neglect of faults in character which it is possible to change?

Let us admit that inheritance forms a large factor in character building. At the same time, be it observed how often the man with a big handicap through inheritance, makes of his life something immeasurably finer than many who are wholly normal. Let it also be recalled that the intellectual part of us is built up entirely during our life-time, and is the product of teaching and training; that our personal power depends on the dominance of intellect over innate or inborn tendencies, and that this dominance is a product of habit, and not an outcome of the capricious summoning of a mighty will. *The will can do but little more than what it is trained to do through habit.*

If we have an unfortunate inheritance, or a particularly bilious temperament, there is all the more reason for discounting our biliousness by acquiring normal habits of mind and conduct. The very thought of abnormal inheritance tends to produce a fatalistic attitude which caters to those weaknesses over which we *have* control. We are endeavouring to develop strength, not weakness, so let us away with thoughts that can do no good, and which tempt us to funk or to excuse undevelopment of stamina in our children.

It is an unfortunate fact that too often heredity is blamed for the inevitable results of the child's imitation of the parents' bad example. What can be expected from a child brought up in an atmosphere of untruth, other than an outlook on life closely related to that of the people with whom it lives? In an infant imitation of feeling rather than of action, is the manner in which the innate tendency operates. Where the babe is subjected to the influence of constant discontent, or frequent wrangling between parents, its natural sunny disposition may, quite possibly, become converted into a so-called "temperament" of gloom.

Although the mind of a babe is quite incapable of reasoning, its impressionability is comparable to that of hot sealing-wax; until chilled by the disillusions of life, either good or bad influences make a deep record upon it. Relying on the unreasoning innocence of a little child's mind, and not realizing its plasticity, an adult, through some act of passion in the child's presence, may create an unfortunate sub-conscious impression which in after years may cause not only peculiarities in character, but serious mental suffering. So it is that we should give our whole attention to those considerations of temperament and mental well-being which lie within our sphere of influence. The training given a child in the first ten years of life is of greater importance than aught else, and the training in the first year, although at the time we fail to see its fruits, counts much more than in the tenth.

Important as these considerations are, it will be realized that to deal with children intelligently, and to adjust our reactions to the impulses they stimulate, generally calls for a lower degree of volition and self-control than is required to promote rational relations with our fellow-men. We are more likely with children to feel our superior power, and to maintain command of the situation, while in our association with adults, our inadequate self-control renders us too often weakly subordinate or vociferously ineffective.

When an animal is baulked in its striving, that is, whenever its wish to act in a certain manner is opposed, its instinct of combativeness is activated, and anger is manifested. In human society, opposition usually takes the form of criticism, and the natural animal reaction to criticism is anger. Further, in human beings there is an innate craving for approbation and sympathy. Failure to receive such is a form of negative criticism which baulks desire, and thereby adds to irritation.

In the jungle, anger, or ferociousness is an effective means for gratifying a desire, or gaining an end; in social life, however, while with timid and weak-minded people anger may appear temporarily efficacious, when it encounters intellect it defeats its own purpose. In all of us there is, when thwarted or criticized, a strong innate animal tendency to become angry, and without the employment of reason, we should soon become our own worst enemies.

In attempting to get our bearings with regard to criticism, let us reflect that none of us is perfect, and that any attempt to keep others from commenting on our imperfections tends to create on their part a desire to break down our foolish resistance. It may be an indication of false pride on the part of people, but the fact is that anything in us which approaches an attitude of all-righteousness, is deeply resented by society, and especially by our relatives. When we seek to prevent others from discussing our actions, this is the attitude we consciously or unconsciously assume.

Free speech or the right to express personal opinion on any matter forms the very basis of freedom, be it national or individual, and many a good man has fought, nay given his life, to uphold it. It is a right which you yourself cherish unless your fear of others renders you silent; it is also a right of others to which your innate tendencies must be made to adapt themselves.

If you admit that you are not perfect, how can you become aware of your imperfections, how advance toward what is perfect, without criticism? Here lies the crux of the whole matter. Do you *wish* to improve? Do you wish to be made aware of your shortcomings? In other words, are you concerned about making the true or rational way of living part of yourself, or is it your desire to be left alone to live as you please, regardless of the truth? You probably answer that you are anxious to follow truth; at the same time, that you wish to do things in your own way.

In what manner does criticism prevent you from doing things in your own way? What is the character of the force which checks you? Is it aught but some fragment of truth contained in the criticism? If it be untruth, what reason to heed it? What we feel to be restricting is not in the criticism, but in ourselves. Through the criticism, a distasteful fragment of truth which interferes with the gratification of our desire, is accentuated in our consciousness and is exposed possibly to the knowledge of other people. Our interrupted desire is in all probability purely self-centered. It may be a wish that our critic should remain either sympathetic to our point of view, or unconscious of our fault. In other words, we are concerned more about appearing right than being right. When we wish above all else to do the *rational* thing, not only do we possess perfect freedom, but another's criticism cannot fail to be helpful. When we consider that a fault discovered to us by one person will probably be perceived and mentioned to ten others by somebody else, we begin to realize the privilege in knowing something of ourselves as others see us. As Burns says:

> "It wad frae monie a blunder free us
> And foolish notion."

The supreme test of your desire for truth is the strength of your wish for those things which elucidate truth, even although they stimulate unpleasant feelings. Of such, criticism is one of the most important. If in your desire to live truly you be quite sincere, you will welcome criticism as a means to that end. If you wish to follow selfish pursuits, or to be considered something you are not, you will never cease to react angrily when, through criticism, these desires are threatened.

You hasten to point out that all this might hold good if criticisms were true, but that very often they are offensive by reason of their falsity. Progress, mental health, and happiness demand the observance of one all-important principle, namely that *attention is to be concentrated on what is true,* and conversely that *what is untrue is to be ignored.* The act of ignoring is essentially negative. If you wish to ignore a person, do you look at him, talk to him, and worry about him? By no means; instead you become particularly interested in some other activity. In the same way, if a criticism be untrue, why give it attention? Perhaps you feel you wish to be regarded in your true light. This is a perfectly legitimate wish, but how best fulfil it? By talking about the untruth, making a fuss about it, and accentuating it, through calling people's attention to it? By no means. Many a man makes a mountain out of a molehill by this very course; and fails to realize that his reaction emanates from false pride, not from self-respect.

Reflect for a moment on your feelings when it happened that another's statement about you was utterly false. You regarded it with equanimity seasoned with humour. Perhaps you felt a little sorry that the other fellow was making such a fool of himself. Subconsciously you felt secure in the knowledge of your integrity. On the other hand, if there happened to be an element of truth, however small, in the statement, your reaction in all probability was considerably more marked. *Whenever you feel particularly annoyed at criticism, search diligently for the element of truth it contains.* A subconscious realization of selfishness is more liable to cause strong reaction than knowledge of virtue.

Another excuse frequently advanced for unbridled reaction to criticism is that it often is delivered in a mean spirit, and with an obvious desire to irritate. Granted that this is so, do you consider such a desire worthy of being gratified? Are you so blind that you do not see the character of the bait, or so easy that you feel compelled to swallow it? Must you always put yourself in another's power, by losing your self-control at a time particularly when you require all your intelligence?

You may not have thought of it in this light. Perhaps you have experienced little of the elation that follows an unsuccessful attempt on the part of another to arouse your anger. If so, know that to remain the custodian of your own emotions when provocation is offered, is a happier and grander experience than to stir the hearts of a multitude. Once you have grasped this idea, you will look for trouble in a way very different from ever before. To be slammed and damned will no longer call forth your abortive retaliation or weak despair; rather will you regard it as one more opportunity to demonstrate to yourself and to others your growing power of adaptation.

When one's mind is full of rational thoughts, it is much easier to cope with what would otherwise hurt. The trouble is we forget so soon to be rational, and spill over with an animal reaction. There is no royal road to success; it comes only by reflecting upon and continually reiterating these and kindred thoughts, until through action in conformity with them we render them a part of ourselves. In this regard success is greatly facilitated by carefully considering the reason for each failure. Every one can recall personal criticisms which, through repetition, have become a "sore point." Why so? Either because we have done our best to correct the criticised fault, or, what is more likely, because we are resistant to criticism as such, and are "not going to be dictated to by other people." We lose sight of the fact that it is not a matter of being dictated to, or of anything other than of what is true.

After the storm of anger has passed, always say to yourself: "This thing, like history, will repeat itself; the next time it comes, how shall I meet it?" To show resistance is to encourage a stronger attack; to meet it by replying: "I shall give careful consideration to what you say," sacrifices no personal rights, gives satisfaction to the critic, is dignified, and affords an opportunity to choose your own time, place, and words in which to pursue the subject further.

While it is important to be able to take criticism intelligently, instead of on feeling, it must be remembered that this, after all, is only the negative side. The ability to point out untruth, or to criticize like a reasonable being, instead of with a display of irritation, is a considerably greater accomplishment. People who dread being criticized, as a rule equally dread offering criticism, and too often find it necessary in order to say what is unpleasant, to work up their emotions to a fighting pitch. If there be a time when one should not offer a criticism, it is when labouring under emotion.

Except when very attenuated, anger interferes with clear thinking, and if one undertakes to set another right, it is his bounden duty to understand clearly what he is talking about.

It is fair to say that in the majority of instances, criticism is but the voicing of a selfish wish. The desire underneath is not so much to be helpful, or to point out the truth, as to gratify a feeling, irrespective of what is rational. When this is the case, criticism is purely a selfish reaction, and the critic can hardly expect to receive respectful consideration.

The test of every criticism lies in whether it be constructive or destructive. If criticism points the way to something better than what is, it is constructive, and should receive commendation and encouragement. If, on the other hand, it merely pulls to pieces, it is what is expressively termed "knocking," and as such should be firmly suppressed. The question is not so much whether a criticism will hurt, because truth always hurts selfishness, but whether it be just, and in support of what is true. Of course one should always seek to hurt as little as possible; no good surgeon is rough; to carry criticism further than the truth demands is harmful.

Before making a criticism, we should ask ourselves what it is we wish to accomplish, and what may defeat our object. If we are content to understate rather than overdraw the unpleasant truth, we shall be more likely to get inside of the resistance which almost inevitably is at first raised. The emotional habit of exaggeration makes it next to impossible for some people to do this.

When, for example, one is accustomed to designate as "absolutely rotten," something which is mildly unpleasant, or to refer in terms of thousands to a matter of tens, it may be taken for granted that there is lacking that close adherence to the truth which makes for all round pleasant association. By giving credit where credit is due we much more effectively overcome resistance. It is seldom that there are not some worthy traits of character, and reference to them when criticizing makes it much more likely that the criticism will receive due consideration.

In our desire to persuade, we are often strongly tempted to overreach the mark, and to try to accomplish the desired end at once by "rubbing it in." If unemotionally presented, truth will reach the mark more directly when left to itself, than when emphasized with irritating insistence. It is most important that we have patience, and not suppose that the good effects of criticism have been lost because a marked reaction follows.

It is almost inevitable that our criticisms will be criticized in none too pleasant a spirit. Quite probably a selfish motive will be attributed to what we have to say. It is because of this that a kindly effort so often degenerates into something akin to a dog fight. Iet us take it for granted before we begin a criticism that we shall receive a sharp or abusive retort. Shall we lose the value of our statement by rushing to our own defence, or by acting truly, shall we be consistent with the truth we are advocating?

Though it might be regarded as fine tactics in politics, in the intimacy of home life, when angry feelings have been aroused, it is no time to push an argument. It is better to wait patiently, and return to the subject when the other's emotional tone gives greater promise of non-resistance. Such a method is persuasion of the highest order, and, provided the criticism offered in this way embody truth, it is bound sooner or later to bear fruit.

A common failing among members of a family is for a critic to take offence if his criticism be unheeded. Anger is a beastly means of accomplishing anything. If a criticism involve a principle essential to rational conduct, the discreet exposure of the point at issue to some one or more respected outsiders will not only require the critic to be pretty sure of his ground, but will put the resistance of false pride where it belongs. The license of familiarity in the home permits a departure from truth that would be amusing were it not the cause of so much avoidable unhappiness. Nothing will send such selfishness scurrying to cover as will exposure, or the possibility of it.

When, in order to avoid imposition in business

relationships it becomes necessary to criticize, it often happens that a person suffers unnecessary nervous excitement, and as a consequence is unfortunate in the type of reaction he stimulates in another. In the regulation of a domestic, for example, both employer and employee often needlessly experience unpleasantness when the former is perturbed, and fails in consequence to have clear cut reasons instead of feelings on which to base the criticism.

The folly of undertaking criticism when annoyed has been considered; the making of the impasse personal, by declaring the offence to be against yourself instead of in opposition to abstract fairness is, also, very unwise. If you be trying to perpetrate anything other than what, on a purely academic basis, is fair and just, it will be difficult to avoid emotion. If your aim be other than single, as for example, to get all you can without incurring a break in relations, you run a great risk of failing in your objective, and of leaving yourself suspended between discontent and fear. Feeling is more contagious than measles, and just the flush on your cheek, if not the tremor of your voice, very often stimulates annoyance in another. Under stress of feeling you will probably over-reach yourself, and exaggerate your claim. It is what is in your heart that is responsible for your perturbation.

On the other hand, if your master-wish be for truth, you do not primarily consider yourself, or any other divergent interests. Your one and only basis of complaint is the infringement of what is fair and just. Anybody's pleasure or displeasure becomes quite a secondary consideration. You know, moreover, what your last word is to be before you utter your first. You realize that, no matter what, for example, an employee's point of view may be, there is no reason to be unsympathetic, and if there be a reaction to your criticism, that is only to be expected in any one whose false pride is touched. When your one desire is fair play all around, you are collected and cool, you have neither hatred nor annoyance in your heart. Consequently, when criticising an employee, you talk with, not at him or her, and question only about what is reasonable—not about what you want.

No matter what his walk in life, the average person has as great a respect for fair play as he has resistance to false pride. If a criticism based on clear-cut right, be resented by an employee, and is the cause of a severance in relations, you should be happy to have it so, for otherwise greater difficulties are certain to arise, and a break in relations sooner or later to become inevitable. When it involves a principle, if you do not intend to act on what you believe to be right, it would be wiser to omit your criticism altogether. So-called "bluffing" is based on untruth. Sometimes it succeeds, but it saps self-respect. No matter what any one else thinks, the bluffer realizes that he has gained his point at the price of false representation, and the price of anything false is extravagantly high. Bluffing does not make for personal power; it entails the same apprehensive nervous strain as any other kind of gambling.

Of all emotional reactions, there are none which can equal in intensity and destructiveness that known as jealousy. Its manifestations in birds and beasts are so generally recognized that comment concerning its innate character is unnecessary. In the human being, when uncontrolled by reason, it occasions such marked functional derangements and absurd conduct that a review of some considerations pertaining to it may be profitable.

Let us suppose that you are the victim of jealousy based not on imaginary, but on actual grounds—the kind of jealousy that popularly is called justifiable. It may be justifiable from man's point of view, but unfortunately that does not render it less disintegrating to your mind or damaging to your body. It might even be of advantage, if it brought suffering to the object of your jealousy, but what is the fact? In that quarter the power it is possible to wield over you, contributes only to egotism, and stimulates a sinister exhiliration.

We have seen in Chapter III that jealousy is a combination of tender emotion, positive self-feeling, anger, and desire for acquisition. This means that, in combination with love, there are three wishes—the wish to be admired by, the wish to hurt, and the wish to possess the object of your jealousy. Obviously the wishes combat each other, give you the pain of the incessant struggle, and of course render you impotent in dealing with the situation. Unless your intelligence intervenes, the mental struggle and pain will continue until one contending faction of wishes dies a natural death.

There are few couples who, on their wedding day, do not earnestly intend to carry out every word of the marriage vow. What happens subsequently to make it otherwise? Serious dissension in a home does not come out of a clear sky any more than hate comes out of sympathy. You have been concentrating your thoughts almost exclusively on the wrong doing of the other. You have been giving your whole attention and effort to the altering of the other's evil ways. You have failed. It was inevitable from the beginning, because you have been working with the wrong person.

Start again, and instead of going over and over in your mind the unfortunate changes which have taken place, and all the cruel things said and done to you since your marriage, consider carefully the changes which have taken place in yourself. During your engagement, you gave promise of many fine traits of character, a cheerful disposition, painstaking care of your personal appearance, sympathy in everyday pursuits, silence in petty follies. Yes, the other has broken down badly; can it be that the chief cause lies in yourself? Can it be that if you had remained true to what *you* promised, the sunshine of life would still fill your home? More important still, can it be that if, in spite of all, you return to the old time sympathetic, cheery ways, you will bring about that which your other methods have failed to accomplish?

You ask: "Would you have me sympathetic with one who is acting in such a way?" Yes, by all means. Once we see in any individual nothing more than his or her wicked ways, we are doomed to become estranged, and cut off from affording help. Where conduct is unwise, by no means show sympathy with its wrongdoing, but never lose sympathy with the individual. There are always extenuating circumstances, and to seek these, and to endeavour to supply the deficiency, should be your constant aim. No one is wholly bad; wickedness is but the correlative of moral weakness. The important point to consider is whether your own actions contribute to another's weakness or strength. The fact that you are jealous shows that you recognize in the other some virtue to admire and develop.

Perhaps you feel it is of no use; that the thing has gone too deep. Consider for a moment the following story: A man owned a garden which might have been beautiful had it not been marred by an immense boulder which reached far under the soil. He tried to blast it out with dynamite, but in the attempt only shattered the windows of his house. Being very self-willed, he used without success one harsh method after another to get rid of the disfigurement until finally he died of worry and blighted hopes. The heir, a man who not only had common-sense, but used it, soon perceived the hopelessness of striving to budge the boulder, and therefore set to work to convert it into a rockery which he covered with frescoes, flowers, ferns, and vines. It soon came about that the visitors to the garden commented on its unsurpassed beauty, and the owner could never quite decide which gave him the greatest happiness, the harmonious aspect of the garden, or his success in adapting himself to the thing that was too deep to move.

If only you will make the effort you can adapt yourself to anything. With jealousy, as with other mental grievances, adaptation lies in getting rid of resistance. In adapting yourself to the wrongdoing of another, remember you make no compromise with evil; you simply find an attitude which enables you to develop, and to benefit by, the other's virtue, without becoming hurt by any element of evil. This can be accomplished only by controlling or renouncing the wishes to hurt, to possess, and to be the central object of the other's affection. In other words, if you can make yourself quite willing to be ignored, if you can go further and find an intense inward satisfaction in your own complacency, you will unfasten the fetters which otherwise hold you in torment.

There is a helplessness and hopelessness about jealousy or grief of other kinds which makes abandonment to it a veritable sin. It rests entirely with yourself as to where you will direct and concentrate your thoughts. Allow your attention to dwell on destructive and grief-laden considerations, and you will suffer tortures; just as soon, however, as you become constructive, and try to develop what is high, instead of accentuating misconduct, your emotional tone becomes joyous, and life takes on a new meaning.

Just as soon as you overcome your resistance—just as soon as you make yourself willing to tolerate the cause of your previous annoyance, a number of surprising things immediately take place. You no longer are held in the power of another. You cease to contribute to vanity by dancing like a puppet to suggestive piping. Your calm indifference to conduct which previously annoyed, and your kindly concern for legitimate needs, accomplish in the other that which no amount of berating could ever have brought about—a blush of shame indicative of repentance. You no longer hate, and suffer the tortures and disability that hatred involves. Your feeling becomes one rather of sorrow for the weakness and suffering that inevitably follow wrong-doing. You will no longer feel the disintegrating weight of self-sympathy, but, in your adaption to what is unworthy, the parts of your personality which otherwise were disorganized and warring, become integrated into a constructive whole, of which the beauty is happiness, and the utility, personal power.

XIX

THE CONTROL OF FEAR

AN outstanding feature of a distraught mind is the dominion of fear and apprehension over the moral self. We call it worry. If there were no personal wishes, the fulfillment of which were regarded as important, there could be no worry. Worry simply is fear that we shall fail to get what we want—fear which turns to pleasure when our desire is fulfilled, or to disappointment, sorrow, or shock, when its fulfillment is denied. It is the suspension between the "I want" and "I may not get" that constitutes worry. Obviously if one could give up the wish, or become indifferent to the outcome worry would vanish.

Some people more than others find it very hard to be denied their wishes; every want assumes an exaggerated importance; consequently every disappointment is proportionately acute. Such persons are chronic worriers, that is to say, they are in a state of chronic fear. They are continually hurting and tiring their bodies by the intensity of their concern in their personal interests. How are they to be relieved?

It is a common misconception to regard idleness or diversion as a cure for a distraught mind.

While in some of the more serious conditions, rest of body, and isolation from new fears and disappointments is essential, it may be stated generally that mental suffering is caused rather by lack of rational mental direction than by mental exertion, and that idleness, far from affording respite, allows the mind to become occupied with self to a harmful degree. If one be suffering from lack of mental control, before starting on the quest for diversion, it might be well to consider whether diversion, or concentration of mind will be the more likely to bring about permanent alleviation of symptoms.

Where mental exhaustion has resulted from forced concentration and mental exertion, rest is of course essential, and a trip to the seaside or some other kind of holiday may afford the recreation necessary. Even in such instances, however, recreation comes, not in causing the mind to become a blank, but in directing it into different and less exacting channels of activity. Diversion as well as concentration can be carried too far. After all, the mind finds greatest rest and, what is more important, satisfaction, through following accustomed lines of activity for four-fifths of one's time.

Individuals whose time is regularly occupied, and whose habits are systematic, have comparatively little opportunity to entertain thoughts which are depressive and hurtful to their bodies. If, however, one be continually rooting up to find some new field of interest, the fatigue incident to change and sight-seeing, and to establishing new relations, coupled with the pernicious effects of incessant irregularity, is worse than staying at home. Far from being less exacting than regular work, such conditions occasion greater confusion and weariness, and, instead of relieving the distressing condition which inaugurated the diversion, add to its intensity and persistence. The power to direct one's thoughts into right channels is not to be found in the unsettled conditions of travel.

We have seen that it is impossible for the mind to concentrate on two thoughts at one and the same time. The cure for irrational fears lies in developing the power of directing the attention, and in strengthening concentration. It is so much easier to take the line of least resistance. The innate tendency, and therefore the natural line of least resistance is to focus the mind on the self, and as surely as one leaves one's thoughts undirected, they will eventually revert to oneself. Further, many a person cannot give overmuch thought to himself without exciting fear—fear of living, fear of dying, fear of his own inadequacy in body, mind, or soul.

There is only one remedy, and it does not lie in smothering one's thoughts by diversion; that is only to put off the issue and to cater to selfish desires. *Control of fear lies in ignoring self through concentrating the thoughts on others.* It is a physical impossibility to entertain at one and the same time fear for ourselves and consideration for another.

Obviously, adequate concern for the needs of others, supported by actual service to them make it impossible for personal fears to dominate the mind.

Suppose your difficulty to be the fear of exerting yourself. You desire to occupy your mind with thoughts of other people, and to render service to them, but your feeling of fatigue makes you afraid of imposing a strain on yourself. If you be timid about overtaxing your body, are you willing to impose a burden on your morale? How much effort have you given to the general practice of renunciation? How many unwise wishes to-day, yesterday, the day before, have you ignored, given up, or in other words, controlled? How often have you over-ridden the desire to sit instead of performing some unpleasant task which you realize your body is quite strong enough to undertake? More important still, how much effort have you made to overcome your fatigue, by refusing to talk about it, sigh about it, write about it, and so on? You cannot forget fear or anything else by making it the subject of your thoughts and actions, even if they be negative.

If you suffer from excess of tiredness, take the following thoughts into consideration. Having no organic trouble, your fatigue is due either to overwork or to auto-suggestion. If it be due to overwork, who do you suggest is responsible? To complain continually of overwork is to indict yourself for irregularity, faulty methods, and poor management. There is no other way of rectifying the difficulty than by giving more careful attention to the control of your twenty-four hours, as practically outlined in Chapter XVI. To do the excess of work which you know is hurtful, and then to complain at the results, is hardly rational.

On the other hand, if you find work distasteful, your tiredness is more likely due to auto-suggestion. After accomplishing a certain amount of work, perhaps a large amount, you subconsciously suggest to yourself that a person having done so much at one stretch, ought to feel tired. You announce that you are tired, you act as though you are tired, and you are tired in your own unchallenged belief.

We all do this sort of thing, some people more than others. It is not the doing of it once or twice that matters, but repetition day after day. When auto-suggestion of this kind becomes a habit, the margin of freshness at work narrows by degrees until even to the victim himself it becomes obvious that the fatigue is quite out of proportion to what it ought to be.

In the early days of your tiredness, had some one challenged your statement regarding your feeling, and called to your mind the fact that the week, the month, or even the year previously, you had accomplished more without fatigue, it may be you would have realized that you were suffering more from a wish for diversion than from actual tiredness. Or even now, should some one suggest just at the time you have come to the conclusion that you are mightily tired, a line of activity in which your enthusiasm is wrapped up, would not the fatigue disappear with your change of mental attitude? Reflect, also, as to whether of late you have allowed the habit of giving in to your wishes or feelings to become more imperative in its demands.

Auto-suggestion with regard to fear of overdoing is much less likely to take root where work has always been clear cut and systematic. If, on the other hand, the work has been more or less optional, you probably have gauged by your feeling of tiredness the amount to be carried out. If feelings were not so subservient to wishes, and consequently sometimes such awful liars, such a method might be practical; the fact is, however, that if you are to act rationally, common sense reasoning, and not a feeling of fatigue or any other feeling, must govern the amount of work it is right for you to undertake.

To regain command of the situation, first obtain expert assurance that there is no organic trouble, then compare your hours of work with those of a normal healthy individual in the same class of society as yourself. The disparity in your hours, and the discomfort you experience, are the result of irregularity and auto-suggestion. Your common sense, if you will listen to it, will tell you how many hours to start with, you should work irrespective of feelings of fatigue. Let this be the standard upon which you build. Realizing that your lassitude is an irrational feeling, and that nothing in the way of illness will result from it, do your best to ignore it, and climb back to the maximum of usefulness, by building each day on the previous day's record.

Make up your mind that you are perfectly willing to feel tired, but that you are neither willing to have it interfere with your usefulness, nor to have your loyalty to duty based on any consideration other than common sense. Realize that whatever pretensions people may make, they and you despise a whiner, and without complaining about it do the thing that will give you new life and vigour. As Professor James says, you soon reach the extremity of distress and then follows unexpected relief, and you get your second wind. If, irrespective of your feelings, you put through each day a carefully prearranged amount of work, your confidence in yourself will quickly return, and it will take but a short time to overcome the persistent auto-suggestion of fatigue which is responsible for the trouble. To ensure success, the activity *must be regular;* nothing should be allowed to make it erratic.

Where there exists a long-standing conviction that work will bring collapse, the situation should be dealt with by a psycho-therapeutist. He will find out what appeals particularly to the patient, and will carefully associate some undertaking with it. In time he will gradually weave more useful activities into the web of the day's pleasurable pursuits, and finally wean the patient from his unfortunate conviction, and so prove to him through his own accomplishments, the irrationality of his fears. In all such cases, to lead gently and firmly is of more avail than to drive. The important thing is to develop the wish in the right direction.

Suppose you suffer from insomnia, and have the fear that inability to sleep will undermine your health. Insomnia is no more serious than the condition which causes it. If it has come about and persists as the result of irregular habits, it would be very foolish to take medicine for it. Medicine which assists a person to defy nature cannot pay in the long run.

No one ever suffered very serious consequences from insomnia caused by lack of nervous control; the discomfort it occasions is the most serious thing about it. If while being regular in your time of getting up as well as retiring, you become willing to endure the discomfort of insomnia, and in this way lose your fear of it, sleep will soon return. It is the inability to ignore a wish that causes the suffering. School yourself in the accomplishment of giving up ordinary unwise wishes, let go those desires which at irregular hours keep you out of bed, or in it, acquire the stamina to suffer in silence, and there will be little difficulty. As Dr. Dubois suggests, sleep is like a coy maiden; court her, and she will keep you courting; cool down, and she will come to terms.

All thought, we have seen, is based on activity of nervous energy paths. Any strong wish augments thought, and stimulates the fear that the wish will not be realized. In general, fear is best controlled by busying the mind with other thoughts; the overcoming of insomnia, however, exemplifies the most negative kind of self-control—a simple letting go of a desire without concentrating the mind in other directions. This can come about only through a willingness to remain awake, which of course means the annihilation of the wish to go to sleep. The willingness to remain awake, furthermore, is not to be fostered by self-entertainment during the hours of wakefulness, as for example by the reading of a novel. The renunciation of the wish to sleep must involve a willingness to lie through weary hours without greater entertainment than that of trying to fall through the mattress. Learn the art of suffering, without advertizing it in any way, and the occasion for suffering will become greatly minimized.

Frequently associated with insomnia, but sometimes distinct from it, is a variety of fear thoughts which you may have experienced, and which, in your more sensible moments, you realize are quite irrational. Your vivid imagination, for example, may picture a street car accident in which your husband is being crushed to death. The howling wind, the rain, or the lightning, contribute possibly to the apprehension. You may allow the mental drama to proceed so far that you grow anxious for your husband's home-coming, and eagerly listen to every sound of his approach. Perhaps you go to the window or to the door time after time to see if he be coming, or, in other ways, work up a harmful degree of fear in yourself.

It is well you should realize that such an emotional pantomime is hysterical weakness. It is simply taking the line of least resistance, and allowing yourself to become the victim of your own suggestion. Of course such phantasies may enter any one's mind, but passively to permit them to take root and grow, to talk, and to act about them, is self-indulgence. When such fears threaten your composure, surely you have some sane peaceful thoughts upon which you can concentrate your mind. It is the ability to command your own attention that requires practice.

Another demonstration of this kind of nervous weakness is found in the foolish fancies of intolerance and incapacity which some people permit themselves to entertain. One person, for example, comes to the conclusion that he cannot tolerate the ticking of a clock on a stand beside him; another that she cannot partake of a meal unless certain flowers on the table are removed; still another that he cannot remain in a house where onions are being cooked. What absurd weakness it is to indulge such caprices!

If your feelings have assumed such a degree of

importance, ask yourself what the difference is between you and other people which will explain this kind of thing. In the past you have always put it down to " nerves "; you realize now that " nerves " is failure of your intellectual self to dominate your feelings. You are suffering from the habit of giving way to your irrational whims. Every one has complexes, including unpleasant associations, which produce whims, but every one does not subordinate his moral self to them. Let it be repeated, to indulge caprice in this way, is to take the line of least resistance. If you fail to over-ride feelings of such insignificance, how can you expect to fare if some really serious discomfort of suffering should overtake you?

Dr. Dubois tells of a wealthy Frenchman whose usefulness was utterly vetoed by his fear or intolerance of noise. Not only did he move from Paris to the country, but he had all the carpets of the house padded, provided sound proof doors, and required the servants to speak in whispers. For a year or more he exhausted the various material methods of medical science in an effort to find relief, but the more attention he gave his weakness, the more pronounced became his suffering. Finally he consulted Dr. Dubois, and received from him the truth as you have received it in these pages. Inside of a week he had returned to ordinary sensible living quarters, and was hard at work in the heart of Paris.

Our tolerance of anything, whether it be disappointment, disaster, suffering, or even death itself, is purely a matter of mental adjustment and adaptation. This can come about only with the realization of the truth—the whole truth, and not just the dark side of it. There never was a misfortune without some redeeming features. It is the wish not to consider the redeeming features, rather than blindness to them, which makes many a man a stranger to happiness.

Why should one not wish to see the advantages in misfortune? Because there is a subconscious wish to obtain from misfortune and misery a distinction or prestige difficult to secure in other ways. Though people may strenuously strive for sympathy, they cannot succeed in making themselves objects of pity without losing something of self-respect. We all seek distinction; let us look for it not in misfortune itself, but in our attitude towards misfortune. The consciousness of being "a quitter" even when there is good excuse, does not contribute to mental health.

Consider as an example, a man who, bed-ridden with organic disease, faces death in a few short months. This is an unfortunate position surely, and it would only raise his resistance to untruth to try to persuade him to other conclusions. That, however, is not the point. The point is that his suffering is no worse than his inability to direct his thoughts. To be sure he has good occasion to enlarge on the distress of his situation, to make things miserably unpleasant for other people, and to develop an appetite for sympathy by making himself an object of pity. Such a course would be the line of least resistance, but what would be the result? Attendants would continue to administer to his needs, not from choice but from a cold sense of duty. The world, which is too ready to shun the unpleasant, would soon forget its privilege of visiting the sick. The tortures of self-pity and fear would soon quite outweigh any physical suffering, and above all, the mental depression that comes with a disintegrating mind would make of an unfortunate situation something appalling and worse than death.

On the other hand, a distinct advantage of illness, misfortune, or disaster, lies in the circumstance that it gives a man a singular opportunity of deriving from the commonplace more than an ordinary amount of self-respect. Possibly you feel that it is not well for a man to be over-burdened with a good opinion of himself. Do not deceive yourself. True self-respect is not the outcome either of material advantage, or of false pride. It is dependent on the strength of the moral self. It is the source of all happiness, and the basis of true conduct. All strive for it with varying success. Many gain the respect of the world, but without realization of moral worth it affords but little happiness. To the man with true self-respect, the opinion of the world is a matter of comparative indifference.

As already pointed out, the animal in man is intimately concerned with material things and pleasures, while the spiritual is wrapped up in thoughts, beliefs, and happiness. The subjugation of the animal part, either through accident or design, is stimulating and developing to the spiritual. The majority of people look at disaster with material eyes. They see only a half truth—the loss of animal gratification and advantage. The other half of the truth is that, much as we dislike being deprived of material possession, there is no doubt that such deprivation rebounds to our spiritual advantage. If, then, we be forced into what is best for us, why should we not season the grief with some appreciation? Why not secure from what the world calls a misfortune the advantage to be derived? Why not willingly sacrifice the pleasures, and reap the superb happiness that triumph of the spirit brings?

If a man have his physical strength, he can reconstruct his material breakdown, and, through the spiritual triumph which such a process calls forth, come out of the disaster a much stronger, more self-reliant and self-respecting man than ever. If, on the other hand, a man resolutely refuses to think of anybody but himself, he will, of course, proceed to develop nervous prostration, will wish to die, and will strive to make his trouble the centre of every other person's attention besides his own.

Consider the effect on self-respect! Everything depends on the way one looks at trouble. Should misfortune and disaster ever come your way, think carefully at the present time, how would you meet it?

To the man who is a victim of prolonged organic disease, exceptional opportunity is given for what the neurologists call "orientation." Such an one, in other words, has a good chance to get his bearings and to adjust his mental compass. Cut off from the daily rush and hurry, protected from those negative features of living which tend to spoil the day's work, and given a simple, regular, circumscribed life, the invalid who fails to secure control of the little that is left, is giving more attention to his loss of pleasure than to his opportunity for happiness.

Where a state of inactivity is irrevocable, the invalid should first of all strive incessantly to extend the renunciation of the unwise wish to those material pleasures of life which are inconsistent with his physical disability. By becoming willing to forego pleasure and sympathy for what he lacks, he will be able to recognize in his situation distinct advantages of a higher type. Secondly, he should make use of every opportunity to develop his advantages for all they are worth. Often he will forget, and, before he is aware of it, find himself whining about some drawback. If necessary, an agreement should be made whereby those about him call his attention to it when this takes place. At first, of course, he will wish to annihilate his prompter; it is, however, with voluntary arrangements of this kind that we gain most quickly the mastery over our hurtful impulses. Where an unfortunate situation can be improved by discussing it, it would be irrational not to do so; it is when we go over and over our irrevocable misfortunes that our lack of adaption to them is rendered painful to ourselves and everybody else.

In illness, as in other misfortunes, the difficulty lies largely in getting rid of resistance, of being willing to be ill. This accomplished, contentment comes unsought and unbidden. A mild feeling of happiness is the natural mental state of every one. It is because the attention is allowed to dwell excessively on thoughts of misfortune to self, that happiness is drowned out.

> "Not by appointment do we meet delight and joy;
> They wait not our expectancy;
> But round some corner in the street of life,
> They, on a sudden, greet us with a smile."

Although all irrational fear is harmful, let us not lose sight of the fact that some fears are not only warranted, but, when combined with volition, afford to mind and body an impelling motive for higher attainment. Ignorance and moral instability are the source of all irrational fear. Not to be afraid of these conditions in ourselves is to live in a fool's paradise. Until false pride and selfishness are eclipsed by humility and love of true conduct, nature will permit irrational fear to haunt the vagrant attention, and drive it back to duty.

XX

ELATION AND PERSONAL POWER

IT has been pointed out that, with animals, pleasant experiences tend to be beneficial, while those of a painful nature are liable to prove detrimental. The same rule applies in a general way to the mind of man. Happy emotional tones are disposed to energize and integrate, whereas painful ones, if permitted, will depress and dissociate. While, as we have seen, intensity of feeling is an important factor in influencing tone—very strong emotion of any kind being unpleasant—the most important factor is the variety of emotions stimulated.

Anger and fear generally produce, like bitterness among the sensations, an unpleasant emotional tone, while elation, which is comparable to the sensation of sweetness, is pleasant. It may readily be understood that it is only by virtue of the contrast that we realize pleasure as distinct from pain, and that a surfeit of the one must result in accentuating the other.

It is a fact that a pleasant emotional tone often accompanies, or temporarily follows irrational conduct. At such times selfish values occupy the larger field of consciousness; later, however, when the mind has become more reflective, and true considerations get their innings, a depressive emotional tone, stronger in its unhappy qualities in virtue of the pleasure which preceded it, takes possession of the mind, and the self suffers in the light of its inferiority.

Like other emotions, elation in the lower animal accompanies many actions, and undoubtedly plays a buoyant part in jungle warfare. In a man whose actions are but feebly controlled by intellect or by æsthetic sense, elation accompanies acts of dominance, oppression, and what is commonly called "putting the other fellow out of business." In some men the instinct of positive self-feeling from which elation springs is so little modified by intellect that they regard it as inconceivable that any one should rise without another's fall. They make the mistake of supposing that Darwin's law of the survival of the fittest applies to intellectual competition as it does to bestial warfare, and they can conceive of no supremacy other than of the type seen in the jungle.

Reasonable considerations, as advanced, for example, in "Industry and Humanity," * make it clear that oppression, let alone the "putting out of business" of any person, works to the disadvantage of the community as a whole. The selfish policy of discouraging anybody in honest effort is but

* "Industry and Humanity," by W. L. Machenzie King, Houghton Mifflin Co.

another indication of the animal disposition little modified by a consideration of truth. Estimated in dollars such supremacy appears to pay, but elation afforded by bestial reaction, sooner or later is followed by a depressing emotional tone which is disintegrating to man's highest faculties, and, for the greater part, renders him a stranger to peace and happiness.

We have seen, on the other hand, that inspiration, of which elation always forms an important part, is capable of influencing the nervous function in ways that to the uninformed appear truly miraculous. It has been shown that a strongly inspirational tone is capable of momentarily restoring the nervous cripple to activity, and of releasing the suffering soul from bondage. There are none of us, moreover, who, when the right stimuli have established cerebral communications with energy levels that lay locked and dormant, have not felt the flood of pent up energies.

If, then, the higher forms of elation are energizing to the body, integrating to the mind, conducive to happiness, and upbuilding to character, by what practical means, and through what stimuli can we bring this emotion into play? As in everything else, there are two sides to the question—a negative and a positive. The vast majority of things, people, and conditions in life possess both elatory and depressing potentialities. The stimulus varies according to the focus of the attention. The optimist devotes his attention unduly to the bright side and stimulates an excessively pleasant emotional tone, while the pessimist goes to extremes on the dark side, and brings about a proportional degree of depression. Both reflect a lopsided impression of truth. Optimism and pessimism are states of mind, not of facts.

It is questionable as to how far the so-called pessimistic temperament is a matter of habit. It is certain that with the *wish* to pull oneself out of the habit of pessimism and despondency, much can be accomplished. It is a matter of placing the attention where it rightfully belongs, and of being honest in giving full credit while pointing out defects.

If you feel unable to direct your attention independently, make an arrangement with those with whom you live to challenge it whenever they hear you talking in a pessimistic vein. As a penalty for having to be checked, force yourself to give voice to an optimistic observation. Gradually your attention will be more and more focused on your weakness until you never forget. By this time you will have realized the positive boost that comes in making encouraging remarks. It not only stimulates your own elation, but the elation you produce in others is reflected.

Some kinds of happy observations stimulate a stronger degree of elation than others, as for example, complimentary remarks to people about their work and character. There never lived a man, woman, or child, who did not possess some accomplishment which deserved commendation. We take it for granted, of course, that everybody, like ourselves, has many points which are anything but commendable, but in developing inspiration it is our business to devote more attention to the all too frequently neglected, optimistic side of truth, and observe silence with reference to unfortunate features we cannot improve.

The reluctance with which people give each other credit for their virtues, and the natural disposition to dwell upon faults, is part of the innate tendency to try to gain personal advantage by trampling on others—a "survival of the fittest" propensity. In social intercourse, where emulation should be the intellectual substitute for pugnacity, it will be realized that to dwell on another's faults is to make oneself the centre of critical inquiry, and a target for retaliation. On the other hand, to make complimentary comment on some point of merit about an adversary, stimulates considerably more elation than the same words applied to a friend. The advice to "love your enemies" is not as wholly idealistic as it seems. To put it into practice by giving full due to your enemy's virtues (for always he has some) and by being silent with regard to his vices, is more than worth while, if only on the basis of benefit to yourself.

When opportunity presents itself to promote

energizing thoughts, unless you have acquired the habit, you will forget to take advantage of the occasion. If, however, you wish to develop your memory more fully in this matter, not only arrange with your closest friends and relatives to check you in a possible tendency to "knock," but make use of a motto, or some such device which will attract your attention each morning, and remind you of your determination. If thus you make it your regular business to start each day by stimulating elation in another, you will not only sow, but will also reap, the inevitably integrating effect that such thoughts and actions have on personality. We best obtain inspiration for ourselves through endeavouring to inspire others.

Even though it be difficult to arouse elation in ourselves to act as though we felt it, that is, to force ourselves to act cheerfully, is the first step in acquiring the habit. It is largely a matter of using volition. It is a habit with some people to be cheerful in all but very exceptional conditions, just as it is habitual for others to be depressing and inconsiderate of the feelings of those about them. Any habit worth forming requires purpose and vigilance, and taking the line of greatest resistance. After all, the mind and the body are not so far apart that they can be out of harmony for any great length of time. Direct your *actions*, your utterances, carefully, and your mind will follow suit; act the part of health and happiness, no matter how you feel, and before long your feelings will harmonize with your actions.

The most constant source of elation is the realization of work well done. To know in your own heart that what you have accomplished is of real value, that it is your best, that you have done it at the expenditure of painstaking volition, is to stimulate feelings that render you at peace with the world and contented in your own mind. The more undeveloped you are, the more you will feel the need of outside commendation; the more, however, you gain confidence in your own knowledge of what is true with regard to your work, the deeper and more independent will be your satisfaction. In this connection, to develop one line of work or one accomplishment until it is outstandingly exceptional, is of greater advantage than to be indifferently equipped along several lines.

In the matter of conferring favours, the opportunity for stimulating elation, or setting free new energy in oneself, as well as in others, is too often degraded into a harmful depressing reaction. When asked to do a thing that you do not wish to do, if you intend to do it at all, that is, if it be right to do it, realize that in it you have a double opportunity of strengthening your personality; first, in the expenditure of volition, to put across wise impulses which are resisted, and second, in the elation the favour, when conferred in the right spirit, is sure to stimulate. On the other hand, to carry out the request in a "confound you" attitude, puts through the disagreeable volitional part of it any way; at the same time, however, the element of hate not only robs you and everybody else of the integrating benefit, but renders the act of small value to others, and disintegrating to your own personality.

In whatever you do, never permit yourself to act on a compulsion basis. If it be rational to do a thing, do it; if it be irrational, refuse to do it, and whichever of the two courses you take, take it in the spirit of an intelligent being, and not with the feelings of a beast of burden. The giving of punctual attention to little things that you intend to do any way for other people, as for example, the paying of bills, the writing of notes of thanks, the calling to express sympathy or appreciation, and so on, sows in the environment seeds of elation, some of the fruits of which you will surely gather.

In his "Memoirs and Studies," (p. 250) Professor William James gives expression to many interesting thoughts on "The Energies of Men." In a charming essay on this subject, which all would do well to read, he says: "The normal opener of deeper and deeper levels of energy is the will. The difficulty is to use it, to make the effort which the word volition implies. But if we *do* make it (or if a god, though he were only the god chance, makes it through us), it will act dynamogenically on us for a month. It is notorious that a single successful effort of moral volition, such as saying "no" to some habitual temptation, or performing some courageous act, will launch a man on a higher level of energy for days and weeks, will give him a new range of power."

Perhaps the highest type of elation is stimulated through a calm and confident adherence to truth in the face of criticism, censure, persecution, and even torture. It is given only to those who have so far developed their self-control that they have broken the bondage of innate desire, and have found their highest heritage in the support of duty at all costs. Such is the power conferred through consistent adherence to what under all varieties of condition is true and rational, that in forces which too often make whining weaklings out of men, one is enabled to find not only triumphant ecstasy, but a means of integrating personality to its strongest development.

Thought is so fleeting that, unless through repetition and action it be developed into conviction, it is driven from the mind by the very circumstances to which it should be applied. Harmonious as may be your wishes with the principles advocated in this book, and determined as you may be at the present time to apply them in everyday living, at the end of a month they will be but an indistinct memory, unless you take some definite measures to make them literally a part of you, unless you have them so at your fingers' ends that they will be automatic in a crisis. To go over them and over them, to talk about them, write about them, tabulate them, develop them by collateral reading, and even to form clubs for their discussion, will consolidate and make them a part of your life. There is no accomplishment more worth while than the accomplishment of self-control.

We all come into the world with unmodified animal instincts and emotions. We have a great heritage of nerve cells through which we can direct and develop paths for impulses which will modify our innate dispositions. Although we may inherit certain tendencies in action, we do not inherit character. Nor do morals descend upon us as a gift from Heaven. Moral perfection is as much an accomplishment of daily effort as is the mastery of engineering, if engineering at its highest can afford a comparison for character.

To say to a man, " love your enemies," when, if angry, he has not enough self-control to give up the wish to do bodily violence, is as impractical as to recite Greek verse to a man who has not acquired a knowledge of the Greek alphabet. He might say he thought it very beautiful, but he would be unable to comprehend the meaning. Except to people most highly developed psychically, the truth that highest happiness lies in service, is likewise as incomprehensible as the beauty of Beethoven is unintelligible to a person possessing a rag-time level of musical appreciation. Unceasing effort and influence will work the change.

Dr. McDougall outlines four levels in moral growth and conduct. At first, the pleasure or pain which accompanies instinctive action affords the sole guide to conduct. Restrictions are imposed on those actions which bring pain, and license is granted to pleasurable activities. A little later, conduct is shaped on the punishment or reward with which it more or less regularly meets. Still later it is obedient to the voice of society—praise and blame, and what people will think. Finally, in its highest development, it is based on an ideal of what is true, and it then is more or less independent of, and unperturbed by the opinions of others.

Every man's life, from beginning to end, calls for constant effort to modify with reason his inborn animal tendencies. The more complex the environment in which he lives, the greater will be the demand on his volition and control. If he becomes lazy, his innate dispositions get the better of him; he loses ability to make correct moral judgments with regard to his own actions, and he loses self-regard. The more he loses self-respect, the more disorganized become his highest faculties.

Self-regard is the source not only of elation, but of volition and control. The more highly a man respects himself, the greater will be his determination to make good in any undertaking, and the more reluctant will he be to give way to unmodified animal reactions. Conversely, the more he bucks into the line of greatest resistance, and the stronger the command he exercises over himself, the greater will be his self-regard. Thus, self-respect, elation, volition, and control, each contributing to the momentum of the other, form the fly-wheel of the mental machinery.

If self-respect be lacking, there is nothing to be gained in self-accusation and remorse—in saying that life has been a failure, and in weakly allowing the self to lie in an inertia of despondency. Such an emotional debauch is further self-indulgence, and the indication is to buck up. It should be a rule never to criticize the past except for the one purpose of seeing where in the future an improvement can be made. There is only one cure for the feelings which give rise to self-denunciation—get busy, do something, develop volition in some way. Effort, and effort alone, can develop accomplishment and ability to serve, and these are the only true grounds upon which to base self-regard.

Let those who are seeking to help in the uplifting of the world realize that constant reviling will foster in others self-disrespect and a "to-hell-with it" attitude. The thing to be sought, found, and developed in people, is their true ground for self-regard. Some basis is always there, possibly buried beneath the wreckage of years, and herein lies the means for augmenting volition. Any one can find sin in another, but it requires the higher qualities in character to discover the virtue. The thing which affords justifiable reason for self-regard—not the wreckage—should be dwelt upon so far as false pride will permit.

We should view the mind as a thing of many parts which requires volition to hold it together. Taking the line of least resistance allows the parts to become loosened and so disorganized that they work to the disadvantage of each other. The effort which is necessary to hold them together, and to make them co-operate to the advantage of the whole, is moral effort—simple obedience to obvious truth through giving up, or letting go, what we know to be unwise, and putting into effect what commonly is called duty. " Duty, though set about by thorns, may still be made a staff, supporting even while it tortures. Cast it away, and, like the prophet's wand, it changes to a snake."

Through obedience to obvious truth, and the integration of character which results, there is acquired the ability to make moral judgment in one's own sphere of experience. Moral judgment merges into intuition, and in a highly integrated character, the degree to which intuition enables one to discern truth and appraise the future appears truly phenomenal.

An unfortunate mistake on the part of many is to regard auto-suggestion as intuition, and, when reacting to the somewhat ridiculous suggestions of their innate dispositions, to flatter themselves on their wonderful intuition. Be it clearly understood that intuition is neither instinct nor reason alone, but the product of all the parts of the personality functioning in harmony. To act without using reason, under the supposition that one is being guided by intuition, is the height of irrationality.

The greater the intellect, the richer is knowledge of experience both personal and of others; and, *provided the knowledge be applied truly,* the more it enhances personal power. By itself, however, intellect is just as capable of operating harmfully as the reverse; to be upbuilding to character it must be integrated with moral stamina.

Where there is good judgment with the moral stamina to act on it, there follows automatically the power of dealing advantageously with varied experiences without being hurt by them—the power of adaptation. There follows adaption, not only to work, play, love, and worship, but to the psychic currents of thought, desire, and persuasion, with regard to truth and untruth alike. To those who lead the simple life, the demands for adaptation are comparatively few, and the development of personality is proportionate. As experiences become more complex, and new demands are successfully met, the greater grows personal power. In the vortex of life's battle, where the stakes are large, and the competition is keen, the demands for adaptation are severe and often cruel. Amid the turmoil of the conflict it is helpful to reflect that we find our greatest strength and highest heritage in adaption to the things we most bitterly resent, and most anxiously would avoid.

The maximum of personal power consists, then, not in strength of body, not in instinct and emotion, not in intellect or reason, not in moral stamina alone, although this is the most valuable of all; it consists in the unification and harmonious working together of each with the other. All can co-operate only through a striving toward the one focus—truth. When each part of the personality is held in its place of relative importance, and there develops a realization of truth in the whole being, "the self," as Dr. McDougall expresses it, "comes to rule supreme over conduct, the individual is raised above moral conflict; he attains character in the fullest sense and a completely generalized will, and exhibits to the world that finest flower of moral growth, serenity. His struggles are no longer moral conflicts, but are intellectual efforts to discover what is most worth doing, what is most right for him to do."

Just in so far as the self is dominated by wishes for what is untrue, it is in bondage; just in so far as it is ruler and not subject of each situation that arises, it has freedom. Until all truth is manifest, and until suggestion ceases to supply untruth with a chimerical halo of attractiveness, men will achieve their greatest personal power through volition and control employed in obedience to duty.

"Stern Daughter of the Voice of God!
O Duty! if that name thou love
Who art a light to guide, a rod
To check the erring and reprove;
Thou who art victory and law
When empty terrors overawe;
From vain temptations dost set free,
And calm'st the weary strife of frail humanity!

. . . .

To humbler functions, awful Power!
I call thee: I myself commend
Unto thy guidance from this hour;
Oh let my weakness have an end!
Give unto me, made lowly wise,
The spirit of self-sacrifice;
The confidence of reason give;
And in the light of truth thy Bondman let me live."

INDEX

Printed in United States of America

For Product Safety Concerns and Information please contact our EU representative GPSR@taylorandfrancis.com
Taylor & Francis Verlag GmbH, Kaufingerstraße 24, 80331 München, Germany

www.ingramcontent.com/pod-product-compliance
Lightning Source LLC
Chambersburg PA
CBHW070822150926
51501CB00043B/944
* 9 7 8 1 1 3 8 5 6 7 3 8 2 *